Montaigne: A Very Short Introduction

VERY SHORT INTRODUCTIONS are for anyone wanting a stimulating and accessible way into a new subject. They are written by experts, and have been translated into more than 45 different languages.

The series began in 1995, and now covers a wide variety of topics in every discipline. The VSI library currently contains over 650 volumes—a Very Short Introduction to everything from Psychology and Philosophy of Science to American History and Relativity—and continues to grow in every subject area.

Very Short Introductions available now:

Available soon:

For more information visit our website

www.oup.com/vsi/

William M. Hamlin

MONTAIGNE

A Very Short Introduction

OXFORD
UNIVERSITY PRESS

OXFORD
UNIVERSITY PRESS

Oxford University Press is a department of the University of Oxford.
It furthers the University's objective of excellence in research, scholarship,
and education by publishing worldwide. Oxford is a registered trade mark of
Oxford University Press in the UK and certain other countries.

Published in the United States of America by Oxford University Press
198 Madison Avenue, New York, NY 10016, United States of America.

© Oxford University Press 2020

Library of Congress Cataloging-in-Publication Data

Names: Hamlin, William M., 1957- author.
Title: Montaigne : a very short introduction / William M. Hamlin.
Description: New York, NY : Oxford University Press, [2020] | Summary: "We
know Montaigne today as the author of a single, extraordinary book: the
Essays. It is a book like no other. People have considered it an
autobiography, a philosophical treatise, and even a Renaissance
self-help manual on how to live, but it is none of these. To be sure, it
offers profound meditations on social and ethical questions, and it
presents one of the most candid self-portraits ever written—a portrait
rich in insight about sanity and peace of mind"— Provided by publisher.
Identifiers: LCCN 2020022937 (print) | LCCN 2020022938 (ebook) | ISBN
9780190848774 (paperback) | ISBN 9780190848798 (epub)
Subjects: LCSH: Montaigne, Michel de, 1533-1592. Essais. | French
essays—History and criticism.
Classification: LCC PQ1643 .H26 2020 (print) | LCC PQ1643 (ebook) | DDC
844/.3—dc23
LC record available at https://lccn.loc.gov/2020022937
LC ebook record available at https://lccn.loc.gov/2020022938

1 3 5 7 9 8 6 4 2

Printed in Great Britain by Ashford Colour Press Ltd., Gosport, Hants.,
on acid-free paper

To the memory of
Shannon Stewart Roberts
(1956–2000)

Contents

List of illustrations

Preface

Michel de Montaigne lived, wrote, and died in sixteenth-century France, but he has long been recognized as a world author: his *Essays* have been translated into fifty languages, and his readers number in the millions. Although conventional wisdom treats him as the founder and first practitioner of the personal essay, this opinion is less relevant to most of us than is the experiential consensus that his book comes as close to being irresistibly readable as any work of prose that survives from Renaissance Europe. Unsystematic in his thinking and unruly in his writing, Montaigne compels our attention through the sense he creates of discovering his views even as he expresses them; no one strikes us as more honest, candid, and spontaneous in his reflections.

Near the end of the *Essays*, Montaigne alleges that "there are more books about books than about any other subject; we do nothing but write glosses about each other." The likely truth of this complaint puts me in a rather awkward position, since as the author of a book on Montaigne I have no choice but to plead guilty to his charge. I will say nonetheless that there is no work I would prefer writing about than the *Essays*, and I feel fortunate to have been able to spend the past few years doing so—not least because my ongoing inclination to read and contemplate Montaigne suddenly coincided with a professional commitment to do precisely that.

This book is intended for a general audience, and particularly for those encountering Montaigne for the first time. I have sought to make it accessible to upper-level undergraduates, to graduate students, and to general readers looking for a broad introduction to the life and thought of the essayist. Ideally it should be read in conjunction with the *Essays* themselves, and in the interests of promoting this possibility I have linked each of my chapters to selected chapters in Montaigne: see the further reading list for specific recommendations. Given that Montaigne is prodigiously quotable, I have quoted him liberally, hoping to provide readers with a well-rounded sense of his voice, style, and characteristic modes of approaching issues and questions. I have attempted as well to convey his irony, humor, and vivid use of metaphor. A different writer would have written a different book; the one I have written concentrates on the topics in Montaigne that strike me as most representative and important for contemporary first-time readers.

An author as forthcoming as Montaigne poses a particular challenge for us: he challenges our imaginations, both biographical and historical. We easily discover what we admire in him—and what seems to anticipate our own attitudes—but we also encounter assumptions and assertions that strike us as uncritical or retrograde, even absurd. I have not avoided or downplayed these features of Montaignian thought. Inasmuch as we cannot form summary judgments about a writer whose work is so vast and demanding, we are encouraged by Montaigne's very complexity to be complex in our own responses, examining our first impressions and visceral reactions within increasingly capacious contexts, many of which are themselves set forth or at least roughly sketched in the *Essays*. We must train ourselves, in short, to move between the local and the global in Montaigne, always remaining open to new avenues of inquiry and new perspectives in interpretation.

My own thinking about Montaigne has been aided by conversation and correspondence with many friends and scholars, among them Warren Boutcher, Alison Calhoun, John Cox, Philippe Desan, Lars Engle, Amy Goldman, Patrick Gray, Patrick Henry, Richard Hillman, George Hoffmann, John Lee, Peter Mack, John O'Brien, Peter Platt, the late Richard Popkin, Amos Rothschild, Richard Scholar, Anita Gilman Sherman, Tim Steury, Richard Strier, and Valerie Worth. More than a few of these people have also written books and articles from which I have learned immensely. Lars Engle, Patrick Henry, Theresa Jordan, Peter Mack, Peter Platt, and Tim Steury took the time to read large portions of this book as I prepared it for publication, and I am indebted to them for their generosity as well as for their probing questions and excellent suggestions for revision. John Snyder provided timely and expert assistance with photography, and Nancy Toff gave me the freedom I sought to individualize this book within the necessary constraints of the Very Short Introduction series. Like most books, this one is finally more collective in its authorship than its title page could ever acknowledge.

But my most fundamental debt is to Montaigne himself, without whose life and *Essays* the world as I know it would be distinctly diminished.

Chapter 1
Writing oneself

We know Montaigne today as the author of a single, extraordinary book: the *Essays*. It is a book like no other. People have considered it an autobiography, a philosophical treatise, and even a Renaissance self-help manual on how to live, but it is none of these. To be sure, it offers profound meditations on social and ethical questions, and it presents one of the most candid self-portraits ever written—a portrait rich in insight about sanity and peace of mind. But the book is more abundant than this. It also constitutes a trenchant assessment of European society from the Greco-Roman era to the French religious wars, and it inaugurates a major new genre of literary composition. Comprising more than one hundred chapters, some short and others very long, the book eschews narrative exposition and provides instead a series of interrelated inquiries into a vast range of topics. Well aware of the idiosyncratic nature of his work, Montaigne describes it as "the only book in the world of its kind, with a wild and eccentric plan" (II.8.278). But he also defends its necessity, claiming that he owes the public a "complete portrait" of himself and that the "wisdom" he proffers lies "wholly in truth, in freedom, in reality" (III.5.677).

Montaigne, then, can be remarkably self-assured, though more typically he strikes us as nonchalant and self-dismissive. Even the title of his book suggests unexceptional aspiration. The French verb *essayer* means "to try" or "to assay," and thus the word

Montaigne selects to describe his musings—*essais*—might be rendered in English as *attempts* or *trials*. As he notes in "Of Democritus and Heraclitus," a crucial chapter that he continued to revise near the end of his life, "I take the first subject that chance offers. They are all equally good to me. And I never plan to develop them completely. For I do not see the whole of anything; nor do those who promise to show it to us....I give it a stab, not as wide but as deep as I know how" (I.50.219). The *Essays*, one might say, are transcriptions of Montaigne's cognitive exercises—of his efforts to penetrate surfaces so as to expose and explore interiors. As such, the book represents not only thought but the sustained observation of thought. It amounts to the collected verbal depictions of an inquisitive, highly independent mind at work.

This is not, however, the way in which Montaigne initially conceived of his project. His early characterizations of the *Essays* often present the book as a token of remembrance for those whom he has known—and an insignificant one at that. "When they have lost me (as soon they must), they may recover here some features of my habits and temperament" ("To the Reader," 2); scribblings like these will "amuse a neighbor, a relative, a friend, who may take pleasure in associating and conversing with me again" (II.18.503). The book, indeed, is a haphazard batch of "absurdities" (I.26.108, II.37.595): the "excrements of an aged mind, now hard, now loose, and always undigested" (III.9.721).

But Montaigne soon discovers that writing can be therapeutic. In a chapter entitled "Of Idleness," drafted shortly after he retired to his rural property at the age of thirty-eight, he relates that when he leaves his mind to its own devices it charges off "like a runaway horse," producing a chaotic sequence of "chimeras and fantastic monsters" (I.8.21). Documenting these phenomena becomes a way of disciplining his intellect, and Montaigne goes so far as to say that he hopes to make his mind ashamed of itself. Perhaps he succeeded. But the cumulative testimony of the *Essays* suggests rather that Montaigne's enterprise led to a progressive diminishment of the very experience of personal shame.

And this brings us to an essential point about Montaigne and his book. However he imagines it when he first begins composing, the idea of self-documentation becomes increasingly expansive over time. Montaigne's insistence that he writes only for family and friends gives way to claims about the inherent value of examining one's consciousness: "There is no description equal in difficulty, or certainly in usefulness, to the description of oneself" (II.6.273). This is not solely because we move thereby toward the Socratic ideal of self-knowledge; an active avoidance of self-deception is equally important. "Those who have a false opinion of themselves can feed on false approbation; not I, who see myself and search myself to my very entrails" (III.5.643–44).

The truth value of essaying is also gradually presupposed. "I expose myself entire," says Montaigne; "my portrait is a cadaver on which the veins, the muscles, and the tendons appear.... It is not my deeds that I write down; it is myself, it is my essence" (II.6.274). We sometimes feel that Montaigne would have proceeded with his book even if there had been no prospect of publication or readership (II.18.504). After all, as Shakespeare put it, "truth is truth to the end of reckoning," and for a man who hated all forms of lying and deception, such an outlook supplies a natural link between living one's life and representing it. "I hasten to bring myself out and put myself forth: I do not want people to be mistaken about me, whether for better or for worse" (II.8.288). Montaigne in fact compares his essay-writing to the Christian devotional practice of conscientious self-disclosure: "In honor of the Huguenots, who condemn our private [Roman Catholic] confession, I confess myself in public, religiously and purely.... I am hungry to make myself known, and I care not to how many, provided it be truly" (III.5.643).

1. This anonymous engraving of Montaigne follows a long tradition of depicting the essayist wearing a neck ruff and a hat; the ruff in particular, due to its impracticality, can be seen as a distinct marker of social status.

This is not to deny that Montaigne creates an authorial persona. All writers do. Montaigne makes deliberate choices about the ways in which he presents himself through language, and readers who spend time with the *Essays* become attuned to his irony and dry humor, his abruptness and restraint, his understatement and hyperbole, and his tactical self-deprecation. But the cultivation of a writerly façade need not diminish the veracity of verbal self-presentation within a sustained piece of prose. Montaigne claims in the preface to his book that had he spent his life in "those nations which are said to live still in the sweet freedom of nature's first laws," he would have portrayed himself "entire and wholly naked" ("To the Reader," 2). But he lived in sixteenth-century France. The linguistic strategies he deploys within the *Essays* thus constitute a finely calibrated means of framing self-disclosure that is at once truthful, arresting, and for the most part tolerable within the culture he inhabits. We must learn to be alert to these strategies, but in the end Montaigne's persona does not betray our trust.

What constitutes truth is the subject of centuries-long philosophical debate—and a question to which we will return in later chapters. Suffice it to say here that Montaigne believes that many truths can be ascertained, not only about the self but about human character and behavior more generally. Yet it scarcely follows from this belief that the results of his investigations amount to teachings that others should adopt. Montaigne is insistent here. "These are my humors and opinions; I offer them as what I believe, not what is to be believed" (I.26.108); "I do not teach, I tell" (III.2.612). During a lengthy trip to Italy in the early 1580s, Montaigne was asked to submit a copy of his *Essays* to Vatican censors for ideological scrutiny (*Travel Journal*, 955–56), and while he largely ignored the changes they recommended, he was more careful thereafter to emphasize his Catholic faith as well as the tentative nature of his ruminations. "I meddle rashly with every sort of subject," he says, but "not to establish the truth," only to "seek it" (I.56.229). "Whoever is in search of knowledge, let him

Writing oneself

fish for it where it dwells; there is nothing I profess less"
(II.10.296).

We see, then, that despite his claims about writing for those who
know him, Montaigne's imagined audience undergoes rapid
expansion, and he soon conceives of readers who will approach his
book with purposes having little to do with its author. In his
brilliant essay "Of Repentance," for example, he concedes that he
sets forth "a humble and inglorious life," but says that this makes
no difference, since we "can tie up all moral philosophy with a
common and private life just as well as with a life of richer stuff.
Each man bears the entire form of man's estate" (III.2.611).
Moreover, and more pragmatically, it occurs to Montaigne that his
writings may possess at least a small degree of social utility. "What
is useful to me might also by accident be useful to another," he
speculates (II.6.272). "The good that worthy men do the public by
making themselves imitable, I shall perhaps do by making myself
evitable.... By my publishing and accusing my imperfections,
someone will learn to fear them" (III.8.703). The extent to which
this claim has proven true is impossible to determine, but it is
fascinating to observe Montaigne's preoccupation with ethically
alert existence and with the idea that his *Essays* might benefit the
world.

In the end, however, the *Essays* are more for Montaigne than for
anyone else: "I feel this unexpected profit from the publication of
my behavior, that to some extent it serves me as a rule" (III.9.749).
In other words, Montaigne's public "confession" obliges him to
stay true to himself and to persist in the path of honest self-
scrutiny. Not only that, but the sustained practice of essaying
ultimately amounts to a form of self-creation. Montaigne is
frequently adamant that the examined life is his specialty—"my
trade and my art is living" (II.6.274)—but he acknowledges as well
that he and his book "go hand in hand and at the same pace.... In
other cases one may commend or blame the work apart from the
workman; not so here; he who touches one, touches the other"

(III.2.611–12). Indeed, Montaigne takes this declaration one step further: "I have no more made my book than my book has made me—a book consubstantial with its author, concerned with my own self, an integral part of my life" (II.18.504). This is a late addition to the *Essays*, a remark coming near the end of a twenty-year span of writing, and it sums up as well as anything Montaigne ever says what he understands his book to be, to do, and to have done.

The inventor of the essay?

To claim that Montaigne invented the essay is like claiming that Joseph Haydn invented the string quartet. At one level the statement is obviously false, but at another it is not merely useful but profoundly true. Everything hinges on definition.

Long before Montaigne, writers in Greco-Roman antiquity had composed prose treatises and dialogues that dealt with historical, religious, and sociopolitical concerns. Plutarch, a Hellenistic Greek whose life spanned the latter half of the first century CE and the first quarter of the second, is famous for writing dozens of moral essays as well as an absorbing set of biographies in which prominent Greek and Roman figures are compared and assessed. Among Plutarch's *Moralia*—his contemplations of social and ethical questions—we find pieces on love, imagination, friendship, the education of children, and many other topics. Montaigne admired these writings and alluded to several of them in his *Essays*, referring fondly to Plutarch's "Opuscules" ("little works") in his chapter "Of Books" (II.10.300). He was also familiar with a tender letter of consolation that Plutarch sent his wife after the death of Timoxena, their two-year-old daughter. Indeed, Montaigne dedicated an edition of this letter to his own wife, Françoise, when their first child, Thoinette, died at the age of two months in the summer of 1570.

Seneca, a Roman statesman, dramatist, and philosopher who also lived during the first century CE, was similarly well known to Montaigne. Of particular interest were Seneca's letters to his friend Lucilius; more than a hundred of these survive. Addressing an enormous range of questions and exploiting the relaxed tonal register enabled by epistolary form, the letters allow Seneca to talk about himself as well as about the concerns of his friend. They thus mix personal anecdote with earnest advice, philosophical disquisition with historical example. The Englishman Francis Bacon, writing in 1612, observed that Seneca's letters "are but essays, that is, dispersed meditations, though conveyed in the form of epistles." In both Seneca and Plutarch, then, Montaigne encountered exceptional models of prose exposition—models embracing the first-person voice and displaying sustained audience orientation through the use of explicit or implied interlocutors. Seneca, says Montaigne, "is full of witty points and sallies, Plutarch full of things. The former heats you and moves you more; the latter contents you more and pays you better" (II.10.301). Montaigne loved them both.

It was not solely in works of antiquity, however, that Montaigne found examples of prose composition that approached his own predilections as a reader and writer. The Renaissance humanist Erasmus—known today for his satirical *Praise of Folly* and his edition of the Greek New Testament accompanied by a new Latin translation—wrote shorter pieces as well, among them an influential discussion of educational theory. This treatise, *On Education for Children*, was itself influenced by the thought of Plutarch. And since education, as we will see, was a subject of consuming interest for Montaigne, it comes as no surprise that in his own essay on the topic he reveals his·acquaintance with several of Erasmus's ideas.

Erasmus was also renowned for a collection of proverbs known as the *Adagia*. Routinely augmented and reprinted, this volume served as a paradigmatic instance of the commonplace book: a miscellany in which insightful quotations from multiple sources could be gathered and organized according to thematic categories. Montaigne informs us that he never kept a commonplace book of his own, and while this is probably true, he was still keenly aware of commonplacing as an educational and heuristic practice. "I go about cadging from books here and there the sayings that please me, not to keep them, for I have no storehouse, but to transport them into this one [the *Essays*], in which, to tell the truth, they are no more mine than in their original place" (I.25.100). This vexed attitude toward the status of borrowed words recurs elsewhere in Montaigne, for instance in his chapter "Of Physiognomy," where he concedes that he has yielded to "the fancy of the age and the exhortation of others" in ballasting the *Essays* with quotations. "But I do not intend that they should cover and hide me; that is the opposite of my design, I who wish to make a show only of what is my own, and of what is naturally my own" (III.12.808).

In one of Montaigne's most extended reflections on his project—a late addition to the essay called "Of Practice"—he claims that contemporary Europeans know the names of only two or three writers from classical antiquity who explored the possibility of verbal self-portraiture. Since then, he adds, no one has followed their lead (II.6.273). The works of these writers have been lost, but it seems improbable that Montaigne would not also have thought of Saint Augustine, whose autobiography, the *Confessions*, constitutes a landmark in the history of life writing. In fact, however, Montaigne never mentions the *Confessions*, and to the extent that Augustine harbors implicit evangelical goals, he treats self-representation in utterly different terms from those adopted by Montaigne. "It is a thorny undertaking," writes the essayist, "to follow a movement so wandering as that of our mind, to penetrate the opaque depths of its innermost folds, to pick out and immobilize the innumerable flutterings that agitate it. And it is a new and extraordinary amusement, which withdraws us from the ordinary occupations of the world, yes, even from those most recommended" (II.6.273).

Here, in the observation and analysis of the meanderings of his mind, Montaigne engages in an activity and a form of writing that strike him as difficult and unprecedented, even "extraordinary." We glimpse his own sense of what he is doing and how he understands it. Returning to our question, then, if we view the essay as a short piece of nonfictional prose that explores a particular topic, Montaigne is certainly not the founder of the genre. But if we view it as a prose composition that makes frequent recourse to personal experience and reflection, tracking its author's attempts to assess what is seen, heard, endorsed, and believed, Montaigne is indeed the first writer to draft such compositions—and on a large scale over a lengthy stretch of time. The Montaignian essay is a form of discourse grounded in the self but never self-indulgent, since its autobiographical dimensions are tactics of enablement rather than gratuitous offerings. And this is why Montaigne can claim that all topics are related: "Let me begin with whatever subject I please, for all subjects are linked with one another" (III.5.668). They are linked because Montaigne's own mind serves as a crucible wherein the swift intercourse between a limitless number of topics is granted original possibility.

Essaying and intimacy

Late in the writing of the *Essays*—sometime after 1588—Montaigne adds a sentence to his already-lengthy chapter "Of Vanity." "Many things that I would not want to tell anyone, I tell the public; and for my most secret knowledge and thoughts I send my most faithful friends to a bookseller's shop" (III.9.750). He is struck, in short, by the irony of this fact—by the unexpected truth that, late in life, he finds himself less constrained in revealing himself to an anonymous audience than in speaking to a trusted companion. It was not always so. Montaigne was fortunate in his younger years to enjoy a friendship of remarkable depth and openness with a man who shared many of his interests. But by the late 1580s that man had been dead for a quarter century, and in the interim Montaigne had published hundreds of thousands of words that, in different circumstances, he might have uttered in private conversation or enclosed within correspondence. He tells us, in fact, that he still holds out hope that his *Essays* will lead to another lucky friendship (III.9.749–50)—and in certain respects they did, though not in a way that Montaigne would have anticipated.

But we must not suppose that Montaigne's "secret knowledge and thoughts" are matters of potential embarrassment. It is the cultural milieu in which he exists that inhibits candid self-expression of the sort he cherishes. Montaigne is impatient with the de facto censorship of customary practice; he loathes dishonesty and self-deception; he is a seeker of communicative intimacy, "hungry" to make himself known. His book thus craves and demands an audience, and for more than four centuries now, readers have willingly accepted the challenge. Perhaps their most common discovery is that in attending to Montaigne they perceive themselves more clearly. As Ralph Waldo Emerson put it in his nineteenth-century essay on Montaigne, "It seemed to me as if I had myself written the book, in some former life, so sincerely it spoke to my thought and experience." Countless other readers have shared this sensation.

Historical assessments of Montaigne's *Essays*

Marie de Gournay, friend of Montaigne and early editor of the *Essays* (1595): "The *Essays* have always served me as a touchstone for testing intellects. I have asked person after person to instruct me as to what I should think of them, so that I might be instructed, according to what degree of worth others saw in them, as to what worth I should see in others."

Sir William Cornwallis, an early reader of Montaigne in England (ca. 1600): "For profitable recreation, that noble French knight, the Lord de Montaigne, is most excellent.... [He] speaks nobly, honestly, and wisely, with little method but with much judgement.... [He] censures and determines many things judicially, and yet forceth you not to attention with a 'hem' and a spitting exordium. In a word, he hath made moral philosophy speak courageously."

William Walwyn, English contemporary of John Milton (1649): "Go to this honest Papist, or to these innocent Cannibals, ye Independent Churches, to learn civility, humanity, simplicity of heart; yes, charity and Christianity."

Blaise Pascal (ca. 1655–60): "That foolish project of Montaigne to depict himself! And this not in passing and against his maxims, since anyone can make mistakes, but through his maxims themselves, by a prime and principal intention. For to say foolish things by accident and through weakness is a common illness, but to say them intentionally is intolerable. And to say such things as these!"

Voltaire (1734): "That delightful project of Montaigne, artlessly to depict himself as he does! For he depicts human nature. And that sad, foolish project of Nicole, of Malebranche, of Pascal, to discredit Montaigne!"

William Hazlitt (1819): "The great merit of Montaigne was that he may be said to have been the first who had the courage to say as an author what he felt as a man. And as courage is generally the result of conscious strength, he was probably led to do so by the richness, truth, and force of his own observations on books and men. He was, in the truest sense, a man of original mind, that is, he had the power of looking at things for himself, or as they really were, instead of blindly trusting to, and fondly repeating, what others told him they were."

Ralph Waldo Emerson (1845): "Montaigne is the frankest and honestest of all writers.... There have been men with deeper insight; but, one would say, never a man with such abundance of thoughts: he is never dull, never insincere, and has the genius to make the reader care for all that he cares for."

Friedrich Nietzsche (1874): "So few writers are honest that we should really distrust all writers. I know of only one writer whom, in point of honesty, I can rank with Schopenhauer, and even above him, and that is Montaigne. That such a man has written truly adds to the joy of living.... If my task were to make myself at home on this earth, it is to him that I would cleave."

Virginia Woolf (1924): "But this talking of oneself, following one's own vagaries, giving the whole map, weight, colour, and circumference of the soul in its confusion, its variety, its imperfection—this art belonged to one man only: to Montaigne.... These essays are an attempt to communicate a soul."

T. S. Eliot (1931): "It is hardly too much to say that Montaigne is the most essential author to know if we would understand the course of French thought during the last three hundred years.... What makes Montaigne a very great figure is that he succeeded... in giving expression to the scepticism of *every*

(continued)

human being. For every man who thinks and lives by thought must have his own scepticism, that which stops at the question, that which ends in denial, or that which leads to faith and which is somehow integrated into the faith which transcends it."

André Gide (1939): "[Montaigne] paints himself in order to unmask himself. And as the mask belongs more to the country and the period than to the man himself, it is above all by the mask that people differ, so that in the being that is really unmasked, it is easy to recognize our own likeness."

Stefan Zweig (1942): "Page after page, I have the impression when I turn to Montaigne that here has been thought, with far more clarity than I could ever muster, all that occupies the most profound recesses of my soul at this moment. Here is a 'you' in which my 'I' is reflected, here the distance between one epoch and another is expunged. This is not a book I hold in my hands, this is not literature or philosophy, but a man to whom I am a brother, a man who counsels me, consoles me, a man whom I understand and who understands me."

Chapter 2
Montaigne's life: a sketch

The first surviving child of Pierre Eyquem and Antoinette de Louppes was a boy whom they named Michel. He was born on February 28, 1533, at Montaigne, the Eyquem seigneurial estate in southwestern France, thirty miles east of Bordeaux. A family of bourgeois merchants, the Eyquems had made their fortune selling salted fish during the fifteenth century, and Michel's great-grandfather, Ramon, purchased the lands of Montaigne in 1477, just eighteen years before the birth of Michel's father. The nobility of the Eyquem family thus derived not from long-standing aristocratic status but from newly acquired wealth, and it was burnished by honorable service in civic and military posts: Pierre Eyquem spent ten years as a soldier in Italy and was later elected mayor of Bordeaux. It was Pierre's eldest son, however, who discarded his father's surname and presented himself instead as Michel de Montaigne.

Antoinette de Louppes, Michel's mother, also came from prosperous mercantile origins. Her extended family, the Louppes de Villeneuve, were well established by the early 1500s as pastel dealers in Bordeaux and Toulouse, and they may have descended from Iberian Jews who converted to Christianity during the previous century. Many such "New Christians" moved to France and the Low Countries around this time, both before and after the forced expulsion of Spain's Jewish populace in 1492. Montaigne says almost nothing about his mother in the *Essays*, but this is more likely due to a difficult relationship with her—and to the bourgeois status of her family—than to her possible Jewish ancestry. Having traded up from "Eyquem" to "Montaigne," the essayist never tells his readers how recently his noble pedigree has been acquired or how closely tied he remains to the nouveaux riches around him. And in any case, his writings show no trace of anti-Semitism, in fact revealing significant curiosity about Jewish cultural traditions. In the diary he kept during his Italian trip, for instance, we read of his visit to a synagogue in Verona and of his attendance at a ritual circumcision in a private residence in Rome (*Travel Journal*, 918, 944–46).

The young Michel had one of the more unusual childhoods known to historians of Renaissance Europe. His father, enamored of humanist optimism and determined to provide his son with every advantage, hired a tutor from Germany who was an accomplished Latinist but spoke no French. Michel thus learned Latin as a first language, claiming in the *Essays* that he was over six years old before he understood "any more French or Perigordian than Arabic" (I.26.128). We sense a whiff of exaggeration here, but it is certainly true that when Michel was later sent to the Collège de Guyenne, an elite boys' school in Bordeaux, he read and spoke Latin so well that he was quickly advanced to upper-level classes despite his relative youth. One result of Pierre's pedagogical enthusiasm, then, was that his son became profoundly bilingual at a time when bilingualism of a lesser caliber was not uncommon. This carried long-term consequences for Montaigne's development as a reader and, ultimately, a writer.

If we trust Montaigne, however, his father may have been disappointed in his son's adult character. Time and again Montaigne informs us that for all the merits of his upbringing, his natural disposition inclines him toward sloth and indecision— though never, thankfully, toward malice. "The danger was not that I should do ill," he writes, "but that I should do nothing. No one predicted that I should become wicked, only useless" (I.26.130). This too may be an exaggeration, for Montaigne seems to have gone on to study law, most likely in Paris or Toulouse. He then served for more than a decade as a case investigator and judicial magistrate in the Bordeaux Parlement—and he almost certainly had higher ambitions than this. But there is no denying that he consistently presents himself as lazy, undisciplined, and disengaged. His father, by contrast, was a man who took pride in managing his lands and who devoted himself unstintingly to his mayoral duties in Bordeaux. Never, says Montaigne, was there "a more kindly and public-spirited soul" (III.10.769).

La Boétie, marriage, and early retirement

It was early in Montaigne's fifteen-year judicial career that he formed an intimate friendship with a young humanist intellectual and poet named Étienne de La Boétie. Slightly older than Montaigne, married, and highly esteemed by his colleagues in Bordeaux's legal establishment, La Boétie was a talented classicist as well as the author of a perceptive analysis of political tyranny, the *Discourse on Voluntary Servitude*. Indeed, it was through the reputation of this book that Montaigne first learned of his future friend: he stresses in his *Essays* that the treatise "was shown to me long before I had seen him, and [it] gave me my first knowledge of his name, thus starting on its way the friendship which we fostered" (I.28.136). Lamentably, however, La Boétie succumbed to a form of dysentery in 1563 at the age of just thirty-two, so this friendship was brutally short-lived. Montaigne describes it in incandescent terms, claiming that "no spoken or written statement in the schools of philosophy ever represented the rights and duties of sacred friendship as exactly as did the practice that my friend and I formed together" (*Travel Journal*, 1060). "If you press me to tell why I loved him, I feel that this cannot be expressed, except by answering: Because it was he, because it was I" (I.28.139).

Prompted by Montaigne himself (III.9.752), scholars have often suggested that the *Essays* owe their existence to the premature death of La Boétie. Abruptly deprived of his dearest friend's companionship, Montaigne turned to pen and ink; his need to communicate remained unchanged, but the hypothetical reader became a surrogate for the deceased beloved. As a theory, this amounts to unfalsifiable speculation, but we should not dismiss it solely for that reason. The idea bears inherent psychological plausibility, and there is no question that Montaigne continued to grieve his friend's absence. In the *Travel Journal*, for instance—a book never intended for publication—we encounter the following entry in May 1581: "I was overcome by such painful thoughts about Monsieur de La Boétie, and I was in this mood so long, without recovering, that it did me much harm" (989). Eighteen years after La Boétie's death, Montaigne still experienced moments of acute longing for his "second self," without whose presence "only half of me seems to be alive" (I.28.143). Grief such as this could surely have channeled itself into sustained efforts at introspective reflection.

We must nonetheless bear in mind that Montaigne led a busy public life between the time of his friend's demise and his own "retirement" in 1571. Besides indulging in various amours and then, at the insistence of his father, agreeing to an arranged marriage in 1565, Montaigne continued to work in the Bordeaux Parlement while simultaneously seeking more desirable employment elsewhere, particularly in Paris and at the royal court. He also supervised the posthumous publication of La Boétie's translations of Greek writings by Plutarch and Xenophon, along with his friend's poems in Latin and French. And, again at the bidding of his father, he undertook a translation of his own: a French rendition of a lengthy Latin treatise by the fifteenth-century Spanish theologian Raymond Sebond. Pierre Eyquem died in 1568 and is unlikely to have seen his son's completed work, but Montaigne published this translation the following year in Paris, calling it *The Natural Theology*. The book is important in its own right, but it plays a critical role in the prehistory of Montaigne's longest and most philosophically oriented chapter, "An Apology for Raymond Sebond."

The woman who became Montaigne's wife, Françoise de La Chassaigne, grew up in a distinguished Bordeaux family and was the daughter of one of Montaigne's colleagues in the Parlement. She was twenty years old at the time of her marriage; Montaigne was thirty-two. Much of what we know about her comes from a series of letters written late in life to her spiritual director in Bordeaux, for she outlived her husband by more than three decades and was known for the austerity of her Catholic devotion during this lengthy widowhood. Earlier, however, between 1570 and 1583, she bore six children, all daughters, only one of whom lived beyond infancy. This was Léonor, born in 1571 and fondly mentioned by her father on several occasions. Françoise, by contrast, receives only slightly more attention in the *Essays* than does her mother-in-law. And yet, as we will see, Montaigne has a great deal to say about marriage and sexuality, much of which is undoubtedly grounded in his experience of conjugal life.

In 1570, frustrated with the legal and religious politics of his job, Montaigne sold his councilorship and retreated to the rural chateau in Périgord where he had been born. There, a few months later, he memorialized his withdrawal from civic activity in a Latin paragraph inscribed on an inner wall of the large stone tower that stood across the courtyard from his house:

> In the year of our Lord 1571, aged thirty-eight, on the day before the calends of March, the anniversary of his birth, Michel de Montaigne, long weary of the court and of the servitude of the Parlement and public offices, still in the prime of life, retired to the bosom of the learned Virgins, where, in peace and security, he shall spend the days that remain to him to live. May destiny allow him to complete this habitation, this sweet retreat of his ancestors, which he has devoted to his liberty, his tranquility, and his leisure.

2. The Château de Montaigne today. The manor house of the original chateau was destroyed in a fire in 1885; it was subsequently rebuilt. But the walls and tower survive largely intact from the time of Montaigne.

Such words sound quite decisive. But in fact Montaigne's retirement from the public sphere had little of the finality implied by this declaration. As his most recent biographer, Philippe Desan, has amply shown, Montaigne continued to harbor hopes of high-profile employment, particularly within the realm of national or international diplomacy. It was nonetheless during the early 1570s that he began drafting the short prose musings that he would later assemble into the *Essays*. He worked for the most part in a circular library on the third floor of his tower, a library that ultimately came to hold about a thousand books, among them those that had belonged to La Boétie, who bequeathed them to his friend at his death (I.28.136; *Travel Journal*, 1050). Montaigne was reading voraciously at this time—in poetry, philosophy, and history, both ancient and modern—and he gradually incorporated hundreds of apt quotations within his writings, usually without attribution. This partly accounts for the hybrid, patchwork quality of the Montaignian essay so striking to first-time readers. It is in any case an essential feature of the genre as Montaigne came to practice it.

Religious warfare, Italian travel, and political life

Throughout Montaigne's adult life, ferocious hostilities between Catholic and Protestant factions raged across France. In Paris during August of 1572, for instance, several thousand Huguenots (French Calvinists) were murdered in the Saint Bartholomew's Day Massacre, and Henri de Navarre—leader of the Protestant cause and future king of France—was seized and placed under house arrest. Montaigne alludes frequently to the civil wars of his time, but he seldom goes into detail, preferring to extrapolate from his knowledge of religiously motivated violence in the interest of exploring alternate modes of behavior. Thus in his famous essay "Of Cannibals," composed during the late 1570s, he juxtaposes contemporary savagery in France against descriptions of ritual cannibalism among Native Americans in what is now Brazil. "There is more barbarity," he concludes, "in tearing by tortures and the rack a body still full of feeling, in roasting a man bit by bit, in having him bitten and mangled by dogs and swine,... than in roasting and eating him after he is dead" (I.31.155). Yet atrocities of the former sort are precisely what France had become accustomed to during its extended, dehumanizing period of religious and political conflict. All through the drafting of the first edition of the *Essays*, Montaigne's ruminations are contextualized by his existence in a war-torn country.

ESSAIS

DE MESSIRE

MICHEL SEIGNEVR

DE MONTAIGNE,

CHEVALIER DE L'ORDRE
*du Roy ,& Gentil-homme ordi-
naire de sa Chambre.*

*LIVRE PREMIER
& second.*

A BOVRDEAVS.
Par S. Millanges Imprimeur ordinaire du Roy.
M.D.LXXX.
AVEC PRIVILEGE DV ROY.

3. Title page of the first edition of Montaigne's *Essais*, published in
1580 by the Bordeaux printer Simon Millanges; the book was released
as a pair of volumes in the pocket-sized octavo format.

That edition was eventually published in the spring of 1580 by a Bordeaux printer and bookseller named Simon Millanges. It was released as a pair of volumes in the small-sized octavo format, the first of these comprising fifty-seven chapters, the second thirty-seven. Montaigne was in his late forties at the time, an experienced husband now, the father of a nine-year-old girl, and a recent victim of the painful malady that had also afflicted his father: the kidney stone. His subsequent journey to Italy between September 1580 and November 1581 was in part an attempt to treat this malady by visiting thermal spas; in his *Travel Journal* he writes in detail about the mineral waters he sips, the time he spends in baths, the color of his urine, and the size and shape of the "stones" that pass excruciatingly through his penis. But it is also clear that Montaigne loved to travel and was eager to examine Roman antiquities and to visit remarkable cities such as Venice, Siena, and Florence. He may, in addition, have been anticipating a diplomatic assignment either in Rome or elsewhere on the Italian peninsula. In the end, however, no such assignment materialized, and Montaigne was instead called back to regional politics in Guyenne, learning in September 1581 that he had been elected mayor of Bordeaux—a post he had never sought.

Returning home, Montaigne assumed his new office with little enthusiasm and spent his first few months preparing a lightly revised version of the *Essays* that appeared in 1582. But at the end of his two-year term he chose to seek re-election. Succeeding in his bid, he found himself increasingly absorbed in local and national politics during the period between 1583 and 1585. Bordeaux, a Catholic and royalist city, was not distant from Protestant strongholds to the south and east, and Montaigne— who by now had earned the respect of King Henri III, Catherine de Médicis (the king's mother), Henri de Navarre, Marguerite de Valois (Navarre's wife), and other figures of great prominence— became much sought after as a dependable and forthright negotiator between Catholic and Protestant camps. An avowed Catholic himself, he maintained cordial relations with a sister and brother who had embraced the Reformed Church, so he knew that confessional coexistence was possible. It was with the reputation of a well-intentioned and pragmatic mediator, then, that Montaigne concluded his mayoralty in 1585 and again retreated to his lands. He was fifty-two years old.

During the first year of this second retirement he seems to have worked steadily on the *Essays*, embarking on a third book to complement the previous two and making numerous revisions to the existing printed text. In 1586, however, the Protestant town of Castillon, just three miles from Montaigne's hilltop home, was besieged by a Catholic army, and Montaigne himself became a target for extremists on both sides. It was probably during this period that the near seizure of the Château de Montaigne took place, an event recorded by the essayist in one of the new chapters he was drafting. A group of thirty armed horsemen gathered in Montaigne's courtyard, claiming to seek refuge from enemy forces, but it soon became clear that this was a ruse and that in fact they were waiting for a signal from their leader—perhaps to hold Montaigne for ransom, perhaps to take his life and seize his money. In the end, their leader changed his mind and led his soldiers away without harming Montaigne or his family. Montaigne, who knew the man, informs us that he later spoke with him about the incident: "He has often said since, for he was not afraid to tell this story, that my face and my frankness had disarmed him of his treachery" (III.12.813). One wonders precisely how to evaluate this remarkable claim.

In addition to being besieged, Castillon was one of several towns along the River Dordogne to be ravaged by the bubonic plague during 1586, and for roughly six months Montaigne was obliged to travel with his family and servants in a sort of refugee caravan, camping at one rural site after another. Only at the end of the year were they able to return to the chateau and take up residential life again. At that point Montaigne must have worked with tremendous speed and self-assurance in drafting the remainder of the *Essays'* third book. This section consists of just thirteen chapters, but they tend to be longer, more personal, and more secure in their views than those in the previous volumes. The Montaigne of Book Three is a man whom fifteen years of essaying have molded into a self-observer of astonishing discernment and finesse.

The final years, Marie de Gournay, and the *Essays* after 1588

Early in 1588, Montaigne traveled to Paris. His trip had multiple purposes, one of which was to arrange for the publication of his new, augmented edition of the *Essays*.

The Parisian publisher Abel L'Angelier undertook this task, producing a handsome quarto volume with an intricately engraved title page and broad margins surrounding the printed text—margins that would almost immediately serve Montaigne as the site for further revisions to his book. A separate and utterly different reason for Montaigne's journey was to act as Henri de Navarre's representative in peace negotiations with King Henri III. Montaigne's intentions in this role are attested to by the English and Spanish ambassadors to France in letters to their respective superiors. Navarre was now the heir presumptive to the French throne, and the king was prepared to meet with him, provided that he renounce his Protestant faith. As it happened, Montaigne was unsuccessful in his mission: the king was forced to leave Paris because of opposition from the Duke of Guise and his ultra-Catholic "Leaguers," and Montaigne was briefly held captive at the Bastille in reprisal for the king's imprisonment of a Catholic extremist in Rouen. Ultimately, the king arranged for the assassination of Guise, and in the following year he was assassinated himself. Navarre thus became Henri IV, the new French monarch. Yet it was only in 1593, four years later, that he finally entered the capital, having announced his

Important early editions of the *Essays*

Essais, 1580: The first edition, printed in Bordeaux by Simon Millanges.

Essais, 1582: The second edition, revised and corrected, with several additions reflecting the concerns of Vatican censors. See, for example, Book One, chapter 56, "Of Prayers" ("Des prières"). Printed in Bordeaux by Millanges.

Essais, 1588: Printed in Paris by Abel L'Angelier, this is the first edition in which the chapters of Book Three appear (thirteen new essays, along with more than 600 additions to Books One and Two). The Bordeaux Copy of the *Essais* is a specific exemplar of this edition, containing extensive manuscript augmentation by Montaigne.

Essais, 1595: Again printed by L'Angelier, this posthumous edition was partly supervised by Marie de Gournay; it is the first to contain the hundreds of manuscript corrections and additions made by Montaigne between 1588 and his death in 1592.

Essayes, 1603: Prepared by the Anglo-Italian scholar John Florio and printed in London, this is the first English translation of Montaigne and the first complete translation of the *Essays* in any language. For his source text Florio relied primarily on the posthumous 1595 edition of the *Essais*.

conversion to Catholicism and allegedly claimed that "Paris is well worth a Mass."

Montaigne, meanwhile, had made an unexpected friendship. In the summer of 1588, he was approached in Paris by an ardent young admirer, Marie Le Jars de Gournay. Only twenty-two at the time, precocious and self-taught, Marie had read the first edition of the *Essays* during her late teens and was hugely impressed by

PATER FAMVLIAM
IPSE VOLLIT

Prophane, ces escrits n'ont qu'un mot à te dire:
Tu n'auraschez-Govrnay que louër ny que lire.

4. Marie de Gournay, from an engraving printed in 1641; Gournay was
Montaigne's most dedicated editor and outspoken proponent during
the early seventeenth century.

the book and its author. Flattered by her interest, Montaigne agreed to visit her at her family's home in Gournay-sur-Aronde, a day's travel north of Paris. He seems in fact to have visited her more than once. The precise nature of his relationship with Marie is a matter of speculation, and it is not unthinkable that the two became intimate, despite an age difference of more than thirty years. What is certain, however, is that Marie de Gournay spent much of the rest of her life promoting Montaigne and his book. She was centrally involved in preparing the first posthumous edition of the *Essays*, published by L'Angelier in 1595, and between then and her death fifty years later, she supervised many additional printings.

In the 1595 text of the chapter "Of Presumption," Montaigne speaks of Marie de Gournay as his "adoptive daughter," adding that he loves her "more than a daughter of my own" and that "she is the only person I still think about" (II.17.502). These lines, however, do not appear in Montaigne's own heavily annotated copy of the 1588 *Essays*, and as a consequence, some scholars have supposed that Gournay fabricated them so as to enhance her reputation. The truth of this matter may never be ascertained. But it is intriguing to note that after Montaigne's departure from Paris in November 1588, he never again saw Marie de Gournay, nor do the two of them seem to have corresponded. Yet upon learning of Montaigne's death a few years later, Gournay traveled to the southwest and spent fifteen months at the chateau, generously hosted, it would appear, by Montaigne's widow and her daughter. By this time Léonor had married, and her first child, a girl, had been christened Françoise. Two decades later, after being widowed and then remarrying, Léonor bore a second child—a daughter she named Marie.

Montaigne stayed close to home for the final portion of his life, never returning to Paris. Two of his letters to Henri IV survive from this period. In one of them, dated January 18, 1590, he tells the king that "I take it as a singular favor that you have deigned to

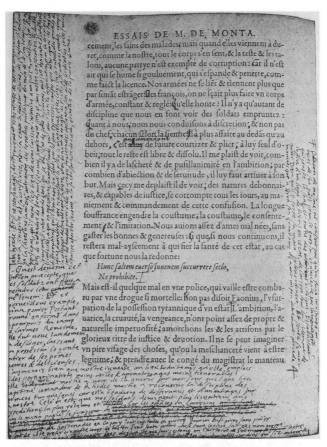

5. An example of Montaigne's handwritten alterations to the 1588 Paris edition of the *Essais*; there are revisions to punctuation and capitalization as well as extensive textual additions in the margins.

make me feel that you would take pleasure in seeing me, a person so useless, but yours even more by affection than by duty" (*Letters*, 1093). From this it would seem that Henri had welcomed the possibility of Montaigne's continued service as an advisor and confidant. But it was not to be. Still plagued by the kidney stone,

Montaigne's health declined, and our knowledge of his continued existence lies primarily in the hundreds of manuscript additions and corrections he inscribed in his copy of the 1588 *Essays*. This "Bordeaux Copy," as it has come to be known, is preserved in the Municipal Library of Bordeaux and regarded as one of the literary treasures of France. But there was evidently another annotated copy of the 1588 *Essays*—a copy used by Marie de Gournay and Abel L'Angelier as they prepared the posthumous edition of 1595. It has now vanished. Had it survived, it would have aided us in making sense of the numerous textual discrepancies between the 1595 *Essays* and various later editions based on the Bordeaux Copy that Montaigne had so copiously augmented.

Textual layers or strata within the *Essays*

The Bordeaux Copy has served as the textual basis for most editions of the *Essays* published during the past hundred years. But from the late sixteenth century until the early twentieth, it was the 1595 Paris edition of Montaigne that functioned as the preeminent source for printed texts of the *Essays*, including most translations (including Florio's). In 1922–23, the French scholar Pierre Villey, relying on the extraordinary editorial labors of Fortunat Strowski, published a three-volume edition of the *Essays* in which he identified the different textual strata comprising the final text of Montaigne's book as represented in the Bordeaux Copy. Thus, according to Villey's system, passages preceded by an "A" (in superscript or within brackets) first appeared in the 1580 or 1582 editions of the *Essays*; passages preceded by a "B" first appeared in 1588; and passages preceded by a "C" constituted manuscript additions in Montaigne's hand that were composed between 1588 and 1592. Subsequent scholars, among them M. A. Screech, have slightly modified Villey's scheme, for instance using "A1" to designate additions first appearing in 1582 after Montaigne's trip to Italy. The following excerpt presents Screech's representation of textual strata within two passages from the chapter "Of Prayers"—a chapter Montaigne continued to revise until the end of his life.

A = Printed text of the 1580 edition

A1 = Printed textual additions first appearing in the 1582 edition

B = Printed textual additions first appearing in the 1588 edition, including all of Book Three

C = Handwritten textual additions within the Bordeaux Copy of 1588

"A1The notions which I am propounding have no form and reach no conclusion. (Like those who advertise questions for debate in our universities I am seeking the truth, not laying it down.) I submit them to the judgement of those whose concern it is to govern not only my actions and my writings but my very thoughts. Both condemnation and approbation will be equally welcome, equally useful, Csince I would loathe to be found saying anything ignorantly or inadvertently against the holy teachings of the Church Catholic, Apostolic and Roman, in which I die and in which I was born. A1And so, while ever submitting myself to the authority of their censure, whose power over me is limitless, I am emboldened to treat all sorts of subjects—as I do here. . . . AWe say our prayers out of habit and custom, or to put it better, we merely read and utter the words of our prayers. It amounts, in the end, to Coutward show. BAnd it displeases me to see a man making three signs of the cross at the *Benedicite* and three more at grace—displeasing me all the more since Cit is a sign which I revere and continually employ, not least when I yawn—Bonly to see him devoting every other hour of the day to Chatred, covetousness and injustice" (I.56.355, I.56.357; cf. Donald Frame's translation, I.56.229, I.56.230–31).

On or around September 10, 1592, Montaigne suffered an abscess of the tongue that inhibited his ability to speak. He may also have undergone a stroke, or perhaps a series of strokes. For the next few days he was forced to communicate by writing notes on scraps of paper. In one of these notes, on September 13, he asked Françoise to summon several of his neighbors, along with his local priest, so that he might hear Mass and say goodbye to his friends. It was during this Mass, at least according to a famous (if possibly spurious) account, that Montaigne, lying in bed, lurched forward with his hands clasped together at the moment of the Host's elevation. At the age of fifty-nine, on the estate where he had been born, in the bedchamber on the second floor of the stone tower where he had written the majority of his *Essays*, Montaigne reached the end of his extraordinary life.

His heart was buried in the parish church near the chateau; the rest of his body was sent to Bordeaux, where it was ultimately interred in the convent of the Feuillants. Montaigne was survived by his wife, his daughter, his infant granddaughter, and also his mother, who lived for another decade and noted her frustrations with her son's estate-management in a will dating from 1597. Antoinette, widow of Pierre, died in 1601 at the age of about ninety years. Her granddaughter Léonor, mother of Françoise and Marie, lived only half that long, passing away in 1616. Françoise, Madame de Montaigne, outlived her daughter by a significant stretch, dying in 1627 at the age of eighty-three. And Marie de Gournay, who had taken it upon herself to ensure that the *Essays* would remain in the public eye, survived their author by more than half a century. Never marrying, she died in Paris in 1645, having lived almost as long since her last encounter with Montaigne as Montaigne himself had lived.

Chapter 3
Learning for living

Enabling his son's exceptional fluency in Latin was not the only parental choice that set Pierre Eyquem apart from his contemporaries. He also arranged for the young Michel to be gently awakened each morning by the sound of a musical instrument—most likely a harpsichord—for he held that "it troubles the tender brains of children...to snatch them suddenly and violently from sleep" (I.26.129). During Michel's infancy, moreover, his father sent him to be breastfed by a woman in a nearby village, and while it was hardly uncommon for an elite family in premodern Europe to employ a wet nurse, Pierre's deeper purpose was to forge a link between his son and the members of the third estate: the peasantry and laborers. "He considered that I was duty-bound to look rather to the man who extends his arms to me than to the one who turns his back" (III.13.844). In essence, Montaigne's father gave him an early lesson in *noblesse oblige*. And it was a largely successful lesson, if we take the son at his word.

Many years later, in the *Essays*, Montaigne offered lessons of his own to various friends and patrons—and to anyone else who might lend an ear. Claiming that "the greatest and most important difficulty in human knowledge seems to lie in the branch of knowledge which deals with the upbringing and education of children" (I.26.109), he set out in multiple chapters to sketch his thoughts on the practices and purposes of learning. As an alumnus of the highly regarded Collège de Guyenne as well as the beneficiary of an extraordinary program of homeschooling, Montaigne was eminently qualified for the task, and his views have been enduringly relevant to teachers and pedagogical theorists, particularly as he formulated them in such chapters as "Of Pedantry," "Of the Education of Children," "Of Books," "Of the Affection of Fathers for Their Children," and "Of the Art of Discussion." Not only does Montaigne raise crucial questions about what, why, and how young people should be taught, but he suggests that the relations between learning and identity are more complex—more problematic and mysterious—than we have traditionally understood them to be.

Teaching, talking, traveling, and truth

In "Of the Education of Children," for instance, Montaigne writes directly to a pregnant noblewoman, the countess Diane de Foix, urging her to take great care in selecting a tutor for the son she is soon to bear (Montaigne feigns certainty that her child will be male). It is not enough, he says, that the boy be taught to repeat the substance of his lesson; he must display "the profit he has made by the testimony not of his memory, but of his life" (I.26.110). In other words, learning must be incorporated within the behavior and character of the learner, and learning that cannot improve a person is unlikely to be worth acquiring. Teachers, meanwhile, are obliged to make sure that their students are given frequent opportunities to exercise their judgment. "Let the tutor make his pupil pass everything through a sieve and lodge nothing in his head on mere authority and trust: let not Aristotle's principles be principles to him any more than those of the Stoics or Epicureans. Let this variety of ideas be set before him; he will choose if he can; if not, he will remain in doubt" (I.26.111).

Doubt, indeed, is a crucial element in Montaigne's educational outlook, and he never strays far from his view that acknowledging uncertainty is one of the surest signs of superior judgment. "Many abuses are engendered in the world," he insists, "by our being taught to be afraid of professing our ignorance and our being bound to accept everything that we cannot refute" (III.11.788). Why not suspend our judgment rather than commit ourselves to accepting or rejecting claims about whose merits we are unsure? "If I had had to train children," says Montaigne, "I would have filled their mouths with this way of answering, inquiring, not decisive—'What does that mean?' 'I do not understand it.' 'That might be.' 'Is it true?'—so that they would be more likely to have kept the manner of learners at sixty than to represent learned doctors at ten" (III.11.788). Inquiry before assertion, debate rather than repetition: these would have been key emphases in the school of Montaigne.

Which is not to say that specific truths cannot be ascertained. Far from it. Montaigne is adamant that all people who engage in discussion—adults and children alike—should be motivated by a desire to discover what is true. The tutor should encourage his pupil "to throw down his arms before the truth as soon as he perceives it, whether it be found in the hands of his opponents, or in himself through reconsideration" (I.26.114). Doggedly defending a false claim is the height of stupidity; changing one's mind is not weakness but strength. Montaigne loved to argue and wrangle—he felt that spirited conversation was "the most fruitful and natural exercise of our mind" (III.8.704)—but he insisted that "the cause of truth" should be the common objective of all disputants (III.8.705). "I give a warm welcome to truth in whatever hand I find it, and cheerfully surrender to it and extend my conquered arms, from as far off as I see it approach" (III.8.705). Resorting in "Of the Art of Discussion" to the same martial metaphor he had used a decade earlier in "Of the Education of Children," Montaigne reveals that while he sees the pursuit of truth as inherently contentious, surrendering himself to indisputable verity is only a figurative defeat; in every important respect it is a victory.

Reimagining one's conversational adversaries as profound philosophical allies is all well and good so long as the individuals in question adopt the same perspective. But frequently they do not. Alert to this unfortunate reality, Montaigne reserves some of his most contemptuous barbs for inept or unyielding interlocutors. "Obstinacy and heat of opinion is the surest proof of stupidity," he writes (III.8.717); "It is impossible to discuss things in good faith with a fool" (III.8.706). At one point he goes so far as to propose that people be fined for adhering to misguided or ridiculous views; this way, at least, a valet could remind his master that "it cost you a hundred crowns twenty times last year to be ignorant and stubborn" (III.8.705). But for all its frustrations, conversation remains for Montaigne a more substantial mode of intellectual engagement than book-learning. "The study of books is a languishing and feeble activity that gives no heat, whereas discussion teaches and exercises us at the same time" (III.8.704). Montaigne was a voracious reader—a man who profited enormously from his sustained exposure to Plutarch, Seneca, Virgil, Horace, Lucretius, and Cicero—so we must set this claim within its proper context and acknowledge its hyperbole. Still, Montaigne is not joking when he says that "if I were right now forced to choose, I believe I would rather consent to lose my sight than my hearing or speech" (III.8.704). Being denied the opportunity to speak his mind and listen to others would have been an excruciating fate for the author of the *Essays*.

Montaigne's attitude toward the reading of books resembles that of Samuel Johnson, the eighteenth-century English lexicographer and editor of Shakespeare. Johnson famously told his biographer, James Boswell, that he seldom read any book from cover to cover: "a man ought to read just as inclination leads him, for what he reads as a task will do him little good." Montaigne, for his part, notes that he leafs "now through one book, now through another, without order and without plan, by disconnected fragments" (III.3.629). And his boyhood experience at the Collège de Guyenne provides an object lesson with respect to Johnson's point about required reading. Despite his outstanding proficiency in Latin, the young Michel was bored by the prescribed curriculum, and it was in large part because he found a sympathetic tutor that he survived his school years as successfully as he did. This tutor, having observed that Michel loved to immerse himself in Ovid's *Metamorphoses*, soon introduced him to other classics, notably Virgil's *Aeneid* and the comedies of Plautus and Terence (I.26.130). Indeed, it may have been through Michel's exposure to ancient drama that he later took pleasure in performing lead roles in Latin tragedies composed by Marc-Antoine Muret, George Buchanan, and other professors at the Collège (I.26.131). Reading and writing were fundamental to Montaigne's existence, and by the end of his life he had composed one of the most original books ever to emerge from Europe, but there is no reason to doubt his repeated insistence that for sheer cerebral exercise, good conversation trumps good reading.

A related point may be made with respect to travel. Even before Montaigne embarked on his lengthy trip to Italy in 1580, he had already accustomed himself to making the most of his interactions with strangers. "In order always to be learning something by communication with others (which is one of the finest schools there can be), I observe in my travels this practice: I always steer those I talk with back to the subjects they know best" (I.17.49). Why ask a German theologian how to manage vineyards in Provence? No doubt he will have an opinion, but do you truly need to hear it? Since the majority of human beings are more inclined to talk than to listen (I.26.113), one might as well encourage them to talk about what they know. And this brings us back to one of the key strategies encouraged by Montaigne in "Of the Education of Children." A tutor should take his pupil abroad as soon as he can, for it is incalculably beneficial to acquire "knowledge of the characters and ways of [foreign] nations, and to rub and polish our brains by contact with those of others" (I.26.112). The pedagogical value of travel—of pure confrontation with cultural and linguistic diversity—cannot be overestimated.

"So many humors, sects, judgments, opinions, laws, and customs teach us to judge sanely of our own, and teach our judgment to recognize its own imperfection and natural weakness, which is no small lesson" (I.26.116). The world is a vast book and, in Montaigne's view, traveling through it and conversing with its inhabitants is just as valid a form of "reading" as is diligent study in a library.

Regrettably, Montaigne lacked the intellectual companionship he would have desired during his lengthy Italian journey (*Travel Journal*, 1014). "It is a rare good fortune," he writes, "to have a worthy man, of sound understanding and ways that conform with yours, who likes to go with you. I have missed such a man extremely on all my travels" (III.9.754). La Boétie comes immediately to mind. But Montaigne made the best of the situation, and his unnamed secretary, who wrote portions of the *Travel Journal*, notes that his master "was so intent on what he encountered, both on the road and at his lodgings, and so eager on all occasions to talk to strangers, that I think this took his mind off his ailment" (*Travel Journal*, 915). It is intriguing to ponder the relations between mind and body suggested by this comment. Montaigne undertook his trip in part to seek relief from the kidney stones that plagued him, but it seems doubtful that he would have sought absolute release from any consciousness of pain. Recalling his oft-quoted exclamation that "it is a wonder how physical [human] nature is" (III.8.710), we are probably right to suppose that momentarily forgetting his "ailment" might have been less desirable than remaining alert to its presence while simultaneously taking pleasure in observing and discussing the unfamiliar.

Interrelations of mind and body are in any case central not only to Montaigne's views on education but to every aspect of his thought about human existence. Running, riding, hunting, wrestling, and dancing should certainly be incorporated within the tutelage of a growing boy such as Frédéric de Foix (for the countess Diane did indeed bear a son). "I want his outward behavior, social grace, and physical adaptability to be fashioned at the same time as his soul. It is not a soul that is being trained, not a body, but a man; these parts must not be separated" (I.26.122). Corporal discomfort will inevitably figure in such training, and in Montaigne's remarks we catch a glimpse of the harrowing realities of life in France during the religious wars. "The boy must be broken in to the pain and harshness of exercises, to build him up against the pain and harshness of dislocation, colic, cauterization, the dungeon, and torture" (I.26.113). In short, he must become acquainted with—if not inured to—forms of suffering to which he may be exposed later in life. But none of this means that the schooling of a youth must ever be accompanied by physical punishment or emotional abuse. Echoing the sentiments of Erasmus, Montaigne condemns all violence "in the education of a tender soul which is being trained for honor and liberty" (II.8.281). Indeed, as we will see, Montaigne's abhorrence of cruelty extends well beyond the confines of home and school. For tutors and teachers, however,

Comments by Erasmus echoed in Montaigne's thoughts on education

"Each species of living creature possesses a common nature; so, for example, the nature of man consists in living according to the dictates of reason. There is also, however, a nature unique to each individual being. . . . Man cannot create or change his natural aptitudes, but, as I have shown, we can reinforce to some extent what nature has given us. . . . Schools have become torture-chambers; you hear nothing but the thudding of the stick, the swishing of the rod, howling and moaning, and shouts of brutal abuse. Is it any wonder, then, that children come to hate learning? . . . Young minds exposed to a congenial program of study that is assimilated in gradual stages and intermingled with play will soon adapt themselves to a more substantial course of learning" (Desiderius Erasmus, *On Education for Children*, 1529).

"severe gentleness" is the ideal instructional demeanor (I.26.122). And while it is entirely appropriate to toughen young bodies, hardening young minds to shame, humiliation, and brutality is criminally indefensible. "Away with violence and compulsion!" (I.26.122).

Learning and the *forme maistresse*

For all Montaigne's emphasis on what might now be called "best practices" in teaching and learning, he was acutely conscious that education is an inherently flawed enterprise and that students respond in different ways to efforts at shaping the mind, body, and character. One can never guarantee, after all, that a given instructor will not be pedantic, manipulative, boorish, or sadistic, and when a classroom is filled with a wide range of pupils it is unreasonable to expect that all of them will thrive. "If, as is our custom, the teachers undertake to regulate many minds of such different capacities and forms with the same lesson and a similar measure of guidance, it is no wonder if in a whole race of children they find barely two or three who reap any proper fruit from their teaching" (I.26.110). But Montaigne was also concerned with a more vexing problem: that of internal, dispositional resistance to external programs of instruction.

This is evident almost immediately in "Of the Education of Children." Asserting that "it is difficult to force natural propensities" (I.26.109), Montaigne implies that teachers and parents cannot blithely trust that the paths they expect young people to follow will in fact be suitable or appealing. As we know, Montaigne was uninspired by the academic program at the Collège de Guyenne, and while he felt as a consequence that he had disappointed his father, he also recognized that his own temperament was significantly to blame. "I was so sluggish, lax, and drowsy that [the teachers] could not tear me from my sloth, not even to make me play.... I had a slow mind, which would go only as far as it was led, a tardy understanding, a weak imagination, and on top of all an incredible lack of memory" (I.26.129). Little wonder that nothing took root in such "sterile and unfit soil" (I.26.129).

Montaignian hyperbole aside, we are nonetheless confronted with our author's evident view that a core of human selfhood exists and that it is essentially indifferent to societal initiatives aimed at fashioning it anew. "There is no one," he says, "who, if he listens to himself, does not discover in himself a pattern all his own, a ruling pattern, which struggles against education and against the tempest of the passions that oppose it" (III.2.615). Drawn from the chapter "Of Repentance," this remark succinctly captures Montaigne's opinion regarding the nucleus of resilient individuality that predates nurture. The key phrase in the original French, *une forme maistresse*, has been variously rendered in English—"a swaying form," "a ruling principle," "a master-form," or, in Donald Frame's translation, "a ruling pattern"—but however it is expressed, the idea is fundamental to the thought of the *Essays*.

Relying in part on the Platonic theory that all earthly phenomena may be understood as imperfect manifestations of original and perfect "forms," Montaigne's sense of this *forme maistresse* is not that of a fixed identity but of an inborn dispositional frame within which specific identity-formations can develop and mature. This frame is neither immutable nor impervious to external influence, but on the whole its boundaries are firm enough to encourage certain long-term tendencies while discouraging others. Montaigne makes frequent attempts to characterize the "ruling pattern" he discovers in himself, and the impression with which we are left is that it privileges several dominant traits that are in turn accompanied by an intricate constellation of aptitudes, tendencies, and quirks. He loves independence, for example; he hates deception and cruelty; he is highly sociable, immune to envy, much inclined to compassion, disinclined to melancholy, uncommonly susceptible to the power of poetry, yet at the same time lazy, irresolute, and impatient with all obligation: "What would I not do to avoid reading a contract!" (III.9.728). Precisely how Montaigne's ruling pattern resists external shaping depends upon specific circumstances; his description of studenthood at the Collège de Guyenne serves well as an illustration. But speaking more generally, he insists that "natural inclinations gain assistance and strength from education, but they are scarcely to be changed and overcome....We do not root out these original qualities, we cover them up, we conceal them" (III.2.615). How they come to be in the first place, and why they are so entrenched, are questions Montaigne does not presume to answer, but he abides firmly by his view that the success of any educational program will always be tempered by those facets of human identity that exist prior to and remain antagonistic toward efforts at reforming their character.

Still, this is no reason not to educate the young. In the best of circumstances, thoughtful training and instruction will help them become not merely more learned, but more astute in judgment, more attentive to virtue, more committed to truth, and more conscious of human frailty. And while Montaigne would have denied that formal education is either sufficient or necessary for wisdom, he would surely have believed that a young person's prospect of growing wise over time can be greatly enhanced by observant, gentle, and life-oriented guidance.

Chapter 4
Friendship, family, love

If we judge Montaigne by twenty-first-century standards of appropriate kinship behavior, we must conclude that he was largely dispassionate about family relations. It is true that he cherished the memory of Pierre Eyquem, "the best father that ever was" (I.28.137, II.12.320), but elsewhere he tells us that he has lost "two or three" children without brooding over their deaths (I.14.42). It is true as well that he refers warmly to his daughter Léonor on several occasions, yet he also says that if she decides in the future that her inheritance is inadequate, "too bad for her; if she is improvident, she will not deserve that I should wish her any more" (III.9.724). Montaigne speaks hardly at all about his wife or his mother in the *Essays*, and while we may partly account for such neglect by acknowledging his era's ubiquitous sexism, we are nonetheless justified in wondering how he could write a lengthy, self-oriented book without mentioning these women more frequently. La Boétie, after all, is quoted multiple times and serves as the focus of two of the *Essays'* chapters, one of them the celebrated discussion "Of Friendship." So how are we to assess Montaigne's views about emotional engagement with other human beings, both within and beyond the domestic sphere? What are we to make of his disparaging comments about women? And how are we to judge his shifting claims on the topics of friendship, love, and sexuality?

"Friendships purely of our own acquisition usually surpass those to which community of climate or blood binds us. Nature has put us into the world free and unfettered; we imprison ourselves in certain narrow districts" (III.9.743). Drawn from the late chapter "Of Vanity," this passage conveys as well as any in the *Essays* Montaigne's overarching assumption about the genesis of interpersonal relations. It is not merely that we choose our friends whereas we are thrown by chance into families and communities; it is also that, broadly speaking, we voluntarily restrict ourselves to the terms and consequences of the latter phenomenon. Yet while Montaigne expresses the same idea in "Of Friendship" (I.28.137), he also contradicts himself by suggesting that his extraordinary intimacy with La Boétie must have been set in motion by some "inexplicable and fateful force" (I.28.139). Whatever the case, both men eagerly sought this intimacy. "Our souls pulled together in such unison, they regarded each other with such ardent affection, and with a like affection revealed themselves to each other to the very depths of our hearts, that not only did I know his soul as well as mine, but I should certainly have trusted myself to him more readily than to myself" (I.28.140).

It is crucial to Montaigne's account of this friendship not only that he and La Boétie were social equals, willing companions, and intensely communicative individuals, but that they were men. "The ordinary capacity of women," after all, "is inadequate for that communion and fellowship which is the nurse of this sacred bond" (I.28.138). Such a view might come as a surprise to the millions of human females who have formed and sustained close friendships down through the ages, but it is an opinion to which Montaigne largely adheres—and to which his classical sources routinely attest. Women, according to the *Essays*, are also more libidinous than men (e.g., III.5.650–59), and they are commonly jealous and obstinate, their "essence" being "steeped in suspicion, vanity, and curiosity" (III.5.662–63). Small wonder, then, that they are incapable of the steadfast, incorporeal mutuality that Montaigne regards as characteristic of the "spiritual" union constituting true friendship (I.28.137).

But there are gaps and inconsistencies in Montaigne's account. For one thing, he admits that the "fleeting affections" of erotic love crossed his consciousness during the time of his friendship with La Boétie—and that La Boétie experienced them as well (I.28.137). For another, he raises the possibility that a heterosexual alliance in which loving amity and corporeal satisfaction were conjoined would be "fuller and more complete" than any other relationship, since it would engage both body and soul (I.28.138). Such a possibility flies in the face of Montaigne's earlier comment that friendship excludes the "fleshly end" of carnal appetite (I.28.137), but as usual we cannot dismiss Montaignian thought on the grounds of self-contradiction. Montaigne is working, slowly and dialectically, toward a more generous understanding of the place of sexuality in human relations. Underexplored and largely undervalued in "Of Friendship," sexual desire returns powerfully to the center of Montaigne's attention in the Book Three chapter "On Some Verses of Virgil."

Before turning to that chapter, however, we must dwell a moment longer on Montaigne's prejudicial contrast between friendship-love and sex-love. The former is characterized by "a general and universal warmth, moderate and even," whereas the latter amounts to "an impetuous and fickle flame, undulating and variable" (I.28.137). In erotic passion, moreover, "there is nothing but a frantic desire for what flees from us," so Montaigne's indictment of sex-love hinges both on its inconstancy and on its intimation of perpetual human neediness (I.28.137). Yet in Montaigne's discussion of "licentious Greek love"—the form of masculine philosophical homosexuality practiced in ancient Athens and famously described in Plato's *Symposium*—he acknowledges that desire can be a path to friendship, and he seems more troubled by the culturally stipulated disparities between the lovers' ages and roles than by their sexual

The vocabulary of friendship and love

Montaigne's essay "Of Friendship" is entitled "De l'amitié" in French. But while *amitié* is the principal French noun for friendship, in Renaissance usage it denotes a wider range of relations than does its modern English equivalent: these include the mutual affection of spouses and the love of parents for children as well as the sort of intimacy Montaigne shared with La Boétie. Meanwhile, the French noun for love, *amour*, is typically reserved in Montaigne's day for erotic relationships between men and women.

"To compare this brotherly affection with affection for women, even though it is the result of our choice—it cannot be done; nor can we put the love of women in the same category. Its ardor, I confess, . . . is more active, more scorching, and more intense. But it is an impetuous and fickle flame, undulating and variable, a fever flame, that holds us only by one corner. In friendship [*amitié*] it is a general and universal warmth, moderate and even, besides, a constant and settled warmth, all gentleness and smoothness, with nothing bitter and stinging about it. What is more, in love [*amour*] there is nothing but a frantic desire for what flees from us" (I.28.137).

Montaigne also alludes to the "four ancient types" of affectionate relations: "natural, social, hospitable, erotic" (I.28.136). He has in mind the traditional taxonomy of love inherited from classical antiquity and laid out, for instance, in Plutarch's dialogue "On Love." The Greek terms *storge* (parental and familial love), *philia* (brotherly love), *agape* (love of one's fellow humans), and *eros* (sexual love) are useful in describing these relations, but Montaigne is well aware that the distinctions between forms of love are not absolute—and that none of these forms is identical to the "real friendship" (I.28.136) he experienced with La Boétie.

involvement (I.28.138–39). All in all, Montaigne's distinctions between love and friendship are neither as sharp nor as convincing as he initially makes them out to be. What is clear, though, is that freedom of choice and equality of status are essential elements in any affectionate union that might approximate the sort of friendship he enjoyed with La Boétie.

Marriage, sex, and sexism

But what about marriage and marital sexuality? Here again Montaigne seems to be of two minds, and in any case unwilling to commit himself to a single, dominant view. In "Of Friendship," for instance, he asserts that marriage "is a bargain to which only the entrance is free—its continuance being constrained and forced, depending otherwise than on our will—and a bargain ordinarily made for other ends" (I.28.137). He later develops this claim in "On Some Verses of Virgil," stressing that "we do not marry for ourselves, whatever we say; we marry as much or more for our posterity, for our family" (III.5.645–46). Freedom is thus largely absent from the "sober contract" that unites men and women for the purposes of procreation and the merging of wealth and property (III.5.645). And this is the sort of contract into which Montaigne had entered with Françoise de La Chassaigne.

To the extent, then, that marriage is a stabilizing social institution, the "extravagances of amorous license" are wholly inappropriate to its ends (III.5.646). As Montaigne notes in the chapter "Of Moderation," the pleasure a husband derives from conjugal relations "should be a restrained pleasure, serious, and mixed with some austerity; it should be a somewhat discreet and conscientious voluptuousness" (I.30.147). No doubt some husbands might have trouble bearing this in mind while engaged in sexual intercourse with their wives, but Aristotle himself corroborates Montaigne's advice, emphasizing that because women are inherently susceptible to lascivious ecstasy, their husbands should caress them "prudently" (III.5.646). In short, erotic love and marital partnership are "intentions that go by separate and distinct roads": "few men have married their mistresses who have not repented it" (III.5.649).

Yet it is precisely within Montaigne's acknowledgment of the constraints and self-disciplinary demands of marriage that he moves toward a more positive estimation of conjugal coexistence. "A good marriage, if such there be, rejects the company and conditions of love. It tries to reproduce those of friendship. It is a sweet association in life, full of constancy, trust, and an infinite number of useful and solid services and mutual obligations" (III.5.647). Montaigne is by no means confident that there are many such marriages, but he knows that there are some, and he implies that marital partners can fashion charitable modes of interaction within the societally determined structures of matrimony. In a post-1580 addition to the essay "Of Three Good Women," for instance, he claims that "the touchstone of a good marriage, and its real proof, is how long the association lasts and whether it has been constantly pleasant, loyal, and agreeable" (II.35.563). Husbands and wives are thus able, by the implied logic of Montaigne's remark, to create the sort of union they wish to share and thereby to approach the conditions of freely elected friendship. Indeed, "it is treachery to get married without getting wedded" (III.5.648), and if friendship of the kind that Montaigne experienced with La Boétie is, by definition, impossible to achieve within heterosexual wedlock, loving companionship founded on mutual respect and generosity is a distinct and realistic prospect.

Whether this was the sort of marriage Montaigne created with Françoise we cannot say. Perhaps at times. He claims, enigmatically, that "licentious as I am thought to be, I have in truth observed the laws of marriage more strictly than I had either promised or expected" (III.5.648). But from the contemplation of his own marital failings it is just a short step to examining the position of women within social arrangements designed by men, and it is here that "On Some Verses of Virgil" yields several of its most perceptive observations. "Women," says Montaigne, "are not wrong when they reject the rules of life that have been introduced into the world, inasmuch as it is the men who have made these rules" (III.5.649). Displaying a remarkable awareness of sexual double standards, Montaigne goes on to illustrate various ways in which feminine gender roles have been shaped and enforced by patriarchal authority. He notes, for instance, that it is "unfair to the ladies to have to lend their lips to any man who has three footmen at his heels, however ugly he may be" (III.5.672). More tellingly still, he writes that "there is hardly one of us who is not more afraid of the shame that comes to him for his wife's vices than for his own" (III.5.655).

Deeply conscious of male hypocrisy within marriage and other social practices, Montaigne nonetheless remains a man of his time insofar as he absorbs and frequently reproduces the misogyny embedded in his culture. Perhaps the most conspicuous example of this may be found in "A Custom of the Island of Cea," where he relates the story of a woman who was gang-raped by a group of soldiers. "God be praised," she is said to have exclaimed; "at least once in my life I have had my fill without sin!" (II.3.257). No doubt this anecdote is proffered mainly as a joke, but Montaigne makes it clear that he believes women experience sexual pleasure even in the midst of violation, and he implies that their wills are thus in partial assent to such transgressive behavior. One wishes he had discussed this matter with his female friends.

Montaigne is also quite severe with regard to wives, despite his willingness to contemplate the possibility of gracious, companionate marriage. Temperamentally inclined to thwart their husbands' desires (II.8.286), wives are capricious and willful, and those who are mothers frequently favor one child over another (II.8.290). The very title of the chapter "Of Three Good Women" is enough to prompt John Florio, Montaigne's first English translator, to rebuke the essayist for misogyny. Writing in 1603 to a pair of married aristocratic ladies, Penelope Rich and Elizabeth

Sidney Manners, Florio states that "this Montaigne-Lord, not so knightly as uncivilly, ... acknowledgeth no dozens of good women at any time in one place... but only a bare trinity." Never mind that Montaigne elsewhere praises many women for courage and marital constancy: Florio is justified in his condemnation. And it is a significant moment in the history of the *Essays*, for it shows that a mere decade after Montaigne's death, a specific male reader is able to step outside his culture's systemic sexism and identify the falsehood of an allegation that might otherwise pass unremarked.

The irony is that Montaigne himself, on multiple occasions, is also able to take this step. Well aware that patriarchal expectations shape women into objects of sexual desire and then condemn them for unchastity, he displays an acute sensitivity to the social construction of gender. He famously concludes "On Some Verses of Virgil" with the remark that "males and females are cast in the same mold; except for education and custom, the difference is not great" (III.5.685). But since we can readily account for the misogyny of men who are raised within the ideological boundaries of a misogynistic world, we are all the more likely to be disappointed in a man who shows the independence of mind to think for himself—yet who nonetheless accepts much of that world's gender prejudice. Montaigne is such a man.

Imagination, pleasure, and children of the mind

As we know, Montaigne is adamant that humans are profoundly "physical" beings (III.8.710). But while this opinion permeates the *Essays*, it acquires particular vigor in Book Three, and yet another remarkable feature of "On Some Verses of Virgil" is Montaigne's astonishing candor about erotic desire—both his own and that of men and women more generally. Early in the chapter he poses the following question: "What has the sexual act, so natural, so necessary, and so just, done to mankind, for us not to dare talk about it without shame and for us to exclude it from serious and decent conversation?" (III.5.644). Later, he provides a partial answer: "Are we not brutes to call brutish the operation that makes us?" (III.5.669). Between and around these remarks he dispenses with conventional propriety and discusses everything from cuckoldry to codpieces, impotence to prostitution, and the "impertinently genital" style in which he arranged his youthful assignations (III.5.679). It is scarcely surprising, then, that the definition of love he eventually offers is ruthlessly demystifying: "I find after all that love is nothing else but the thirst for sexual enjoyment in a desired object, and Venus nothing else but the pleasure of discharging our vessels—a pleasure which becomes vicious either by immoderation or indiscretion" (III.5.668).

But sex-love is more complex than this, and Montaigne knows it. As he notes in a lengthy post-1588 addition to the chapter "Of the Power of the Imagination," our bodily members do not always cooperate with our carnal intentions. The penis in particular insists on its own "unruly liberty" with regard to performative expectations (I.21.72–73). Still more intriguingly, sexual arousal is tightly bound up with the ways our minds are disposed to perceive the activities in which our bodies are engaged. A woman might sleep with one man while fantasizing about another: "What if she eats your bread with the sauce of a more agreeable imagination?" (III.5.673). And men would do well to allow their lovers to bring them circuitously toward sexual consummation. "We should take pleasure in being led there, as is done in magnificent palaces, by divers porticoes and passages, long and pleasant galleries, and many windings" (III.5.671). Obstacles, frustrations, resistance, and pain can likewise intensify erotic satisfaction. Montaigne in fact devotes an entire chapter to this idea ("That Our Desire Is Increased by Difficulty"), but in "On Some Verses of Virgil" he presents it in its most elemental context. "Love," he says, "is founded on pleasure alone, and in truth its pleasure is more stimulating, lively, and keen [i.e., than that of marital affection]: a pleasure inflamed by difficulty. There must be a sting and a smart in it. It is no longer love if it is without arrows and without fire"

(III.5.649). The assertion, then, that love amounts merely to the gratification of sexual desire is repeatedly qualified by the *Essays* as a whole.

To return, then, to where we began—with the domestic realm of family relations—we would be remiss not to acknowledge that Montaigne exhibits a degree of emotional detachment that strikes many modern readers as eccentric or peculiar, perhaps even offensive. At times this detachment is colored by attitudes that derive in part from ancient Stoicism, as when Montaigne writes that "we should have wife, children, goods, and above all health, if we can; but we must not bind ourselves to them so strongly that our happiness depends on them" (I.39.177). Elsewhere it seems grounded in mature self-knowledge, if tinged as well with wry humor: "The commonest and healthiest sort of men consider an abundance of children a great happiness; I and some others regard the lack of them as equally fortunate" (I.14.42). This latter remark is a late addition to the *Essays*, a sentence drafted after 1588 when Montaigne's wife Françoise was in her mid-forties and unlikely to conceive again, so we might justly ask whether Montaigne is making a virtue of necessity. Perhaps he might have felt differently had he fathered a son. At all events, near the close of the chapter "Of the Affection of Fathers for Their Children," he makes the case that books are children too (II.8.291–93). He acknowledges that his ruminations in prose are scarcely in the same league as Virgil's poetry, but he has given them what he could, "as one gives to the children of one's body" (II.8.293). He claims, moreover, that "I do not know whether I would not like much better to have produced one perfectly formed child by intercourse with the muses than by intercourse with my wife" (II.8.293).

One wonders whether Françoise or Léonor ever read this sentence—and, if so, what they felt or thought about it. Our understanding of their emotional lives, not to mention that of Montaigne himself, would be richer for the knowledge.

Chapter 5
Free and sociable solitude

That solitude nurtures liberty and that public life impairs it are ideas for which one may find immense support in the *Essays*. Yet Montaigne repeatedly troubles this opposition, suggesting that levels of personal freedom are not as closely correlated to differences between public and private engagement as one might initially suspect. Indeed, the conventional rigidity of the public/private distinction is partly eroded by Montaigne, with the result that we risk misrepresentation if we hold uncritically to the long-standing view that the essayist, in retreating to his tower and library, secured the liberation from worldly affairs that constituted an essential prerequisite for writing his book.

The early essay "Of Solitude" is significantly responsible for this view. Among Montaigne's many assertions here is that the happiness of adults should not depend on emotional bonds to spouses or children. He then adds this: "We must reserve a back shop all our own, entirely free, in which to establish our real liberty and our principal retreat and solitude. Here our ordinary conversation must be between us and ourselves, and so private that no outside association or communication can find a place" (I.39.177). Because Montaigne owned a manor house on a large rural estate, readers new to the *Essays* sometimes miss the figurative nature of this claim, and Montaigne may invite confusion inasmuch as he famously describes his tower's alluring privacy in another, later essay, "Of Three Kinds of Association":

> When at home, I turn aside a little more often to my library, from which at one sweep I command a view of my household. I am over the entrance, and see below me my garden, my farmyard, my courtyard, and into most parts of my house. There I leaf through now one book, now another, without order and without plan, by disconnected fragments. One moment I muse, another moment I set down or dictate, walking back and forth, these fancies of mine that you see here. It is on the third floor of a tower; the first is my chapel, the second a bedroom and dressing room, where I often sleep in order to be alone. Above it is a great wardrobe. In the past it was the most useless place in my house. In my library I spend most of the days of my life, and most of the hours of the day. (III.3.628–29)

Montaigne's comment in "Of Solitude," however, is resolutely metaphorical. As he says elsewhere, noting that he views his home as a refuge from the political turmoil of France, "I try to withdraw this corner from the public tempest, as I do another corner in my soul" (II.15.467). And this latter "corner" is Montaigne's "back shop": a state of tranquility derived from self-respect and trust. "Let us make our contentment depend on ourselves; let us cut loose from all the ties that bind us to others; let us win from ourselves the power to live really alone and to live that way at our ease" (I.39.177).

It would be easy to accuse Montaigne of complacent elitism given the nonchalance with which he adopts a project of self-dependence and worldly withdrawal. Important critiques in this vein have in fact been published. But Montaigne is always conscious of his privileged social status. As he notes with respect to a related concern—his hatred of being obligated—"I try to have no express need of anyone.... This is a thing that each man can arrange for himself, but more easily those whom God has

54

6. Montaigne's three-story tower, from outside the wall of the chateau's inner courtyard; it was in a circular room on the third story of this tower that Montaigne kept his books and did much of his writing.

sheltered from natural and urgent necessities" (III.9.740). More to the point is that Montaignian solitude is never a matter of escapism. "We have a soul that can be turned upon itself; it can keep itself company; it has the means to attack and the means to defend, the means to receive and the means to give: let us not fear that in this solitude we shall stagnate in tedious idleness" (I.39.177). As with the project of the *Essays* as a whole, withdrawal from society for the purposes of self-regard is a legitimate undertaking, neither vain nor frivolous, and in Montaigne's estimation distinctly more respectable than such worldly choices as the pursuit of reputation or glory.

But it is precisely here that "Of Solitude" tends to encourage a less social vision of privacy than Montaigne generally endorses. In an extended rebuttal of what he views as the hypocrisy of Cicero, who retired from public life only to seek renown through authorship, Montaigne assembles a selection of vivid quotations from Seneca:

> It is a base ambition to want to derive glory from our idleness and concealment. We must do like the animals that rub out their tracks at the entrance to their lairs. Seek no longer that the world should speak of you, but how you should speak to yourself. Retire into yourself, but first prepare to receive yourself there; it would be madness to trust in yourself if you do not know how to govern yourself. There are ways to fail in solitude as well as in company. (I.39.182–83)

Retirement, by this account, entails discipline; we must respect, cherish, and carefully manage ourselves without desiring worldly recognition. But in the Book Three essays that Montaigne drafted after his tenure as mayor of Bordeaux, we find a new dimension to this account, one hinted at in "Of Solitude" but more vigorously presented in "Of Husbanding Your Will," a chapter that may be viewed as a companion piece to the earlier essay.

"My opinion is that we must lend ourselves to others and give ourselves only to ourselves," says Montaigne (III.10.767). Another way of putting this is that our lives in the public sphere are like theatrical roles: "We must play our part duly, but as the part of a borrowed character. Of the mask and appearance we must not make a real essence" (III.10.773; cf. III.2.613). Shakespeare presents the same idea in *As You Like It*: "All the world's a stage, / And all the men and women merely players." But in Montaigne the idea is more complex because it is linked to a dialectical conception of selfhood. Only through proper attention to oneself can one effectively approach societal engagement. Being one's own best friend and observer is the key to successful involvement in external affairs. Such a person, "knowing exactly what he owes to himself, finds it in his part that he is to apply to himself his experience of other men and of the world, and, in order to do so, contribute to public society the duties and services within his province" (III.10.769).

Montaigne, incidentally, is well aware of the distinction we now draw between introverted and extroverted personalities. He is quick to acknowledge that "there are private, retiring, and inward natures" (III.3.625). But his own "essential pattern" is communicative and unreserved. "I am all in the open and in full view, born for company and friendship. The solitude that I love and preach is primarily nothing but leading my feelings and thoughts back to myself, … I throw myself into affairs of state and into the world more readily when I am alone" (III.3.625). He is, in short, an extrovert who seeks solitude in society and society in solitude. The two states complement one another, and Montaigne's desire to sequester himself does not conflict with his fundamentally expansive nature. In a letter composed in February 1585 to Jacques de Goyon-Matignon, marshal of France, Montaigne stresses that "I shall never cast myself back into solitude so far or unburden myself of public duties so thoroughly as not to retain a singular devotion to your service and a fondness for being wherever you may be" (*Letters*, 1081). Elsewhere, referring to his mayoralty, he states that "I have been able to take part in public office without departing a nail's breadth from myself, and to give myself to others without taking myself from myself" (III.10.770). Indeed, he suggests that the best leaders and civil servants are those who can steer clear of passionate involvement in the matters with which they must deal (III.10.770–71).

Montaigne, then, does not equate solitude with aggressive or uncompromising withdrawal. His solitude is both social and sociable, restorative for the self and imperative for public engagement. As the scholar George Hoffmann has written in a fascinating study of the ways that Montaigne's authorial career depended on unremitting social interaction, we should not imagine the essayist as nestled in solipsistic isolation: "Montaigne instead regarded solitude itself as a social act, a way of positioning oneself inside of society, 'alone in a crowd.'"

Liberty and its infringements

Liberty is never far from the center of Montaigne's attention. We have seen that he regards a concern with personal independence as one of his chief traits (III.9.759)—unquestionably a component of his "ruling pattern"—and in his final chapter, "Of Experience," he writes that "I am so sick for freedom, that if anyone should forbid me access to some corner of the Indies, I should live distinctly less comfortably" (III.13.820). Throughout the *Essays* he is extraordinarily alert to the means by which individual or collective forms of liberty may be compromised. But broadly speaking, it is in his earlier writings that he displays the greatest confidence that human beings are free agents who can exercise their wills in accordance with the dictates of rational deliberation. Later, this confidence undergoes significant qualification.

Initially composed around the same time as "Of Solitude," the chapter entitled "That to Philosophize Is to Learn to Die" offers an optimistic account of our ability to confront mortality on our own terms. "It is uncertain where death awaits us," writes Montaigne; "let us await it everywhere. Premeditation of death is premeditation of freedom. He who has learned how to die has unlearned how to be a slave. Knowing how to die frees us from all subjection and constraint" (I.20.60). Montaigne, it should be noted, is not presenting an argument for suicide (although he is not categorically opposed to the idea); he is proposing, rather, that through steady contemplation of death we can eliminate its strangeness and terror. And such contemplation lies wholly within our choice. We can likewise diminish the debilitating effects of pain: we have the power "to lessen it by patience, and, even should the body be disturbed by it, to maintain nevertheless our soul and reason in good trim" (I.14.38). We sense little intimation here of the inseparable union of mind and body that Montaigne stresses so emphatically elsewhere.

A different perspective on this early Montaignian confidence may be seen in the brief chapter "That Intention Is Judge of Our Actions." Here Montaigne is acutely conscious that we cannot control the outcomes of our choices, and as a consequence we should only be judged on the basis of our intentions: "there is nothing really in our power but will" (I.7.20). Precisely what Montaigne's intentions were a decade later when he served as mayor of Bordeaux seems to have been a point of controversy among his contemporaries, some of whom thought that he behaved "like a man who exerts himself too weakly and with a languishing zeal." Indeed, Montaigne admits that these critics were "not at all far from having a case" (III.10.781). But he stresses in the same crucial chapter that he would have worked more assiduously "had there been any great need of it. For it is in my power to do something more than I do or like to do" (III.10.781). Even in the mid-to-late 1580s, then, Montaigne still insists that his will is his own and that he could have acted otherwise than he did had he so chosen.

We must nonetheless set these expressions of confidence against a pervasive Montaignian awareness of the ways in which life and society encroach on personal liberty. A list of such infringements would include, at the very minimum, age, chance, habit, family circumstance, state of bodily health, local custom, individual temperament, cultural expectation, zealous commitment to a cause, and adherence to a particular metaphysical system. No doubt there are others. Even the mutability of human consciousness erodes the firmness of the will: "We float between different states of mind; we wish nothing freely, nothing absolutely, nothing constantly" (II.1.240). But one of the most fascinating forms of infringement lies with involuntary preference, especially the "fortuitous instinct that makes us favor one thing more than another and that assigns us, without leave of our reason, our choice between two like objects" (II.12.425). Montaigne's English contemporary Francis Bacon would have classified this "instinct" as one of his "Idols of the Tribe," an element within the makeup of human subjectivity that conditions behavior and militates against the meticulous "true induction" that Bacon so earnestly recommends. In any event, Montaigne memorably exemplifies this instinct in the late chapter "Of Physiognomy": "in a crowd of victorious enemies you will instantly choose, among men unknown to you, one rather than another to whom to surrender and entrust your life" (III.12.811). It seems probable that he speaks from harrowing personal experience.

But it is the chapter "Of Repentance" that offers the most powerful discussion of the limitations of human freedom. Having argued elsewhere that social existence inevitably forces us to subordinate our individual desires to those of the group (III.5.648, III.9.758), Montaigne now asks whether the socially sanctioned view of repentance in his culture has any bearing on one's identity and volitional status. "My actions," he writes, "are in order and conformity with what I am and with my condition. I can do no better. And repentance does not properly apply to the things that are not in our power; rather does regret" (III.2.617). His conscience, he adds, is "content with itself" (III.2.612), and if he were to live his life again, he would live as he has lived already (III.2.620). His guiding premise is that people behave in accordance with the ways in which they are constituted. They discover who they are just as much as they create who they are. To speak, therefore, of repenting actions or behavioral patterns that we have consciously willed, perhaps for many years, comes close to being oxymoronic. We might even say that Montaigne articulates an ethical stance wherein one may be fully guilty of a particular act without being fully responsible for it. It is at any rate the case that by the time he writes "Of Repentance," Montaigne displays an understanding of human liberty far more somber than that presented in the first edition of the *Essays*. And solitude has little to do with this altered view.

"The freedom of our soul"

The greatest value of solitude may lie in its capacity for sharpening our habits of perception. As Montaigne notes in "Of Custom, and Not Easily Changing an Accepted Law," "the wise man should withdraw his soul within, out of the crowd, and keep it in freedom and power to judge things freely" (I.23.86). It is true that Montaigne goes on to recommend that this man conform to accepted norms of behavior, but such conformity can readily coexist with private judgments that stand in opposition to prevailing social practice. Not surprisingly, one of Montaigne's most illuminating comments on this perceptual duality appears in "Of Husbanding Your Will":

> The mayor and Montaigne have always been two, with a very clear separation. For all of being a lawyer or a financier, we must not ignore the knavery there is in such callings. An honest man is not accountable for the vice or stupidity of his trade, and should not therefore refuse to practice it: it is the custom of his country, and there is profit in it. We must live in the world and make the most of it such as we find it. But the judgment of an emperor should be above his imperial power, and see and consider it as an extraneous accident: he should know how to find pleasure in himself apart, and

to reveal himself like any Jack or Peter, at least to himself.
(III.10.774)

For an emperor to regard his power as an "accident" is to
acknowledge that things might be otherwise than they are. There
is nothing necessary or inevitable about such power—or about any
state of human affairs—and it is a mark of wisdom to keep this
fact continually in mind. The emperor, moreover, should strive to
know who he is without his imperial trappings and to enjoy the
presence of his own unsponsored being. Solitude can help with
this. It can stave off the self-neglect to which most people are
prone when immersed in public activity.

For Montaigne, then, both internal and external perception can be
enhanced through the discipline of solitude. And social
detachment need not be literal. We can retreat to our "back shop"
even in the midst of business. It is a matter of not forgetting
ourselves, of acknowledging our "essential pattern" (III.3.625), of
resisting the self's openness to colonization from without, and of
retaining as sharply etched a sense of identity as is possible given
the concurrent reality of unending change. Is this self-love?
Presumably so. But it is not the self-love so shrewdly explored
during the following century by François de La Rochefoucauld in
his famous *Maxims*, for while it is no doubt rooted in a healthy
regard for the ego, it strives consistently to avoid the twin hazards
of self-worship and self-deception. To be sure, the efficacy of
Montaignian solitude depends on routine detachment from
custom, community, family, and friends, but its inestimable value
lies in the sanity and balance with which it sends us back to them.

Chapter 6
America

Montaigne never uses the word *America*. Like many of his contemporaries, he speaks of the "New World" or the "Spanish Indies" when he refers to the lands of the Western Hemisphere. But America is very much on his mind in the *Essays*. Two of his chapters, "Of Cannibals" and "Of Coaches," are primarily devoted to New World concerns, and several others offer intriguing comments about Native American peoples, particularly with respect to their cultural practices and their interactions with Europeans. Montaigne is deeply interested in these peoples; he learns a good deal about them by reading histories of the French colonial enterprise in Brazil and the Spanish conquests of Mexico and Peru. But America's inhabitants also serve him in a distinctly polemical fashion. Their cultures, collectively considered, become a near-utopia against which European society is set to conspicuous disadvantage. Montaigne's America is not only a site of extreme cultural difference but an archetype of natural simplicity by means of which the essayist can meditate on barbarism and civilization, cruelty and courage, and the ancient opposition between art and nature.

For a brief period during the late 1550s, French settlers led by Nicolas de Villegaignon attempted to establish a permanent colony along the Brazilian coast near what is now Rio de Janeiro. They called it "Antarctic France" (I.31.150). In 1560, Portuguese forces destroyed the colony's principal outpost on the island of Serigipe, but some of the French escaped to the mainland, where they continued to live among the local populace. It was not until 1567 that French activities in this region were finally suspended, and even after that France engaged in sporadic colonial ventures along the eastern seaboard of North and South America, not surprisingly ignoring the Treaty of Tordesillas in which Spain and Portugal had agreed to divide the lands of the New World exclusively between themselves.

Montaigne tells us in "Of Cannibals" that one of his former servants had lived for a decade in Antarctic France. "A simple, crude fellow" (I.31.151), this man was allegedly incapable of embellishing his travel stories, and as a consequence Montaigne regarded him as a particularly trustworthy source about New World ways of life. The man also introduced Montaigne to sailors and merchants he had met during his time in the colony, and it was perhaps through this network of acquaintance that Montaigne acquired various American artifacts, including hammocks, wooden swords, percussion instruments, and poems (I.31.154–58). Some years earlier, in the autumn of 1562, Montaigne had met and spoken with several Brazilian natives who had been brought to Rouen for display before Charles IX, the adolescent king of France. Montaigne's American knowledge, then, was not solely derived from books; his country's colonial ambitions gave him inadvertent access to more direct forms of testimony regarding the vast world on the far side of the Atlantic.

And it is within this context that we must read "Of Cannibals," for Montaigne places special emphasis on information he has gathered through personal inquiry. Speaking of the Tupinamba natives of coastal Brazil, he makes the following memorable claim:

> I think there is nothing barbarous and savage in that nation, from what I have been told, except that each man calls barbarism whatever is not his own practice. Indeed it seems we have no other

test of truth and reason than the example and pattern of the
opinions and customs of the country we live in. *There* is always the
perfect religion, the perfect government, the perfect and
accomplished manners in all things. Those people are wild, just as
we call wild the fruits that Nature has produced by herself and in
her normal course; whereas really it is those that we have changed
artificially and led astray from the common order, that we should
rather call wild. (I.31.152)

The Tupinamba, as we subsequently learn, are cannibalistic—they
eat the flesh of their captured enemies as a form of "extreme
revenge" (I.31.155)—but Montaigne finds their cannibalism less
troubling than the ways in which Europeans typically generate
allegations of savagery. Unfamiliarity, he suggests, is the principal
criterion by which most people form such judgments: a practice is
savage if it fails to cohere with one's cultural expectations. But in
making this claim, Montaigne shrewdly relies on the twin
denotations of the French adjective *sauvage*, which means both
"savage" and "wild." The Tupinamba are *sauvages* in essentially the
same way that uncultivated fruits are *sauvages*: they have not
been subjected to domestication. Montaigne thus engineers a
revaluation of savagery while at the same time positing a
comparative cultural chronology in which Native Americans
represent a phase of human existence much closer to "original
naturalness" (I.31.153) than that of their counterparts in the Old
World.

But they are not in a state of prelapsarian innocence. Montaigne is
clear about this. The Tupinamba still engage in "the human
disease" of warfare (I.31.156), and at one point, after observing a
particularly gruesome form of vengeance practiced by the
Portuguese, they adopt it on the grounds that it is "more painful
than their own" (I.31.155). Montaigne's claim is not that Brazilian
natives are noble savages but that they are far less savage than
their European contemporaries. "I am not sorry," he says, "that we
notice the barbarous horror of such acts, but I am heartily sorry

65

7. Tupinamba natives (in what is now Brazil) taunt a defiant enemy prisoner as they prepare for his ritual execution; later they will eat him. Montaigne discusses this scene in his essay "Of Cannibals" (I.31.155).

that, judging their faults rightly, we should be so blind to our own" (I.31.155). Writing in 1579, when French religious conflict has persisted for more than fifteen years, Montaigne is depressingly familiar with the betrayals, deceptions, and atrocious acts of violence committed by his countrymen on both sides of the Catholic-Protestant divide. American cannibals may be barbaric with respect to "the rules of reason," but French antagonists in Montaigne's own day surpass them "in treachery, disloyalty, tyranny, and cruelty, which are our ordinary vices" (I.31.156).

In essence, Montaigne interprets the very fact of *difference* between the New World and the Old as a tension between natural and artificial behavior. The nudity of American natives is literal, but for Montaigne it is figurative as well: it signifies their freedom from the needless encumbrances of European life, and thus their comparative purity. Europeans, meanwhile, are beset with superfluous desires, and their laws, hierarchies, and technological adaptations constitute a fundamental corruption of that which is natural and pristine. This is not to deny that hammocks and poems are works of human artifice; Montaigne knows this. But on his imagined scale between natural simplicity and debased complexity, the "knowledge of how to enjoy [one's] condition happily" (I.31.156) lies almost entirely with the naked cannibals of America.

On the October day in 1562 when Montaigne found himself in the presence of several such cannibals, someone asked them what they regarded as the most striking features of French society. They said, first, that they thought it "very strange" that so many armed and powerful men would "submit to obey a child"—King Charles being only twelve years old at the time (I.31.159). Strange, too, was the fact that the poor and the hungry among the French population preferred to live in misery rather than rebel against their affluent fellow citizens. If La Boétie had still been alive he would have found these observations surprisingly pertinent to his arguments in the *Discourse on Voluntary Servitude*. In any event, once the king had left the premises, Montaigne at long last had an opportunity to speak directly with an American native. And though his incompetent translator misunderstood much of what Montaigne wanted to say, he managed to ask this man what privileges he enjoyed as a military figure. The American replied that he was thereby enabled to lead an army of four or five thousand warriors and to walk through jungle underbrush on paths prepared for his comfort. Montaigne was impressed. "All this is not too bad," he wrote, clearly praising the cannibals. "But what's the use? They don't wear breeches" (I.31.159).

Virtue, vice, and cruelty

If Montaigne relies on trenchant irony as he closes his chapter "Of Cannibals," he prefers a tone of calm earnestness in "Of Cruelty," an essay in which he lays out sharp distinctions between goodness and virtue before identifying cruelty as "the extreme of all vices" (II.11.313). Alluding to the idea of natural propensities—an idea on which he routinely depends—Montaigne writes that in his opinion "virtue is something other and nobler than the inclinations toward goodness that are born in us" (II.11.306). Many people, Montaigne among them, are predisposed to a mild benevolence, experiencing no desire to harm others or to indulge in serious forms of vice. But is this virtue? Montaigne thinks not. A man who forgives an insult because he has an easygoing nature must be judged quite differently from a man who chooses forgiveness after resisting a passionate urge for vengeance. "One action might be called goodness, the other virtue. For it seems that the name of virtue presupposes difficulty and contrast, and that it cannot be exercised without opposition" (II.11.307).

So far, then, so good. But in one of the *Essays'* great examples of thought in motion, Montaigne turns to contemplate the lives of Socrates and Cato the Younger. He cannot believe that either of these men was forced to struggle against vicious appetites and passions. Their virtue was not laborious but customary, the product of exceptional inborn character enhanced by "long exercise in the precepts of philosophy" (II.11.310). Virtue, for them, had become second nature, and their habituation to its dictates was so complete that the slightest stirrings of vice were immediately extinguished in their souls. Moral excellence was their normative condition.

Montaigne thus develops an ethical taxonomy in which his own modest goodness exemplifies the least evolved of three species. "Accidental and fortuitous" (II.11.311), his virtue is the luck of birth combined with strong modeling by an exemplary father. But it is not therefore despicable. At the very minimum, Montaigne can boast that he holds most vices "in horror" and that he has felt this way throughout his life (II.11.312). Indeed, he goes so far as to remark that, on the whole, his behavior is more admirable than his thinking: "I find in that area, as in many things, more restraint and order in my morals than in my opinions, and my lust less depraved than my reason" (II.11.312). This is a post-1580 addition to "Of Cruelty," a sentence first appearing in the 1588 *Essays*, and one is tempted to wonder which (if any) of the numerous views expressed in Book Three represent "opinions" for which

Montaigne now chastises himself. One thing is clear: whatever they might be, they are unlikely to deal with cruelty.

For cruelty is the vice he hates the most. Speaking of his natural tendency to sympathize with those who suffer, Montaigne writes that "the dead I hardly pity, and I should rather envy them; but I very greatly pity the dying. Savages do not shock me as much by roasting and eating the bodies of the dead as do those who torment them and persecute them living" (II.11.314). Once again we have a juxtaposition of New World natives against Old World barbarians. And while it is true that cruelty was never regarded within Christianity as one of the Seven Deadly Sins, for Montaigne this does nothing to mitigate its abhorrence. His essay "Of Conscience" exposes contradictions embedded within the European reliance on judicial torture, and in "Cowardice, Mother of Cruelty" he explores the validity of the proverbial claim that it is not courage but its absence that draws people into gratuitous and sadistic violence.

Montaigne on torture (from "Of Conscience")

"Tortures are a dangerous invention, and seem to be a test of endurance rather than of truth. Both the man who can endure them and the man who cannot endure them conceal the truth. For why shall pain rather make me confess what is, than force me to say what is not? And on the other hand, if the man who has not done what he is accused of doing is patient enough to endure these torments, why shall the man who has done it not be also, when so fair a reward as life is set before him? . . . To tell the truth, torture is a means full of uncertainty and danger. What would a man not say, what would a man not do, to escape such grievous pains? . . . Whence it happens that the man whom the judge has tortured so as not to make him die innocent, is made to die both innocent and tortured" (II.5.266).

Just as there are congenital leanings toward goodness, moreover, there are innate seeds of brutality: "Natures that are bloodthirsty toward animals give proof of a natural propensity toward cruelty" (II.11.316). And such propensities can be strengthened through custom and habituation (I.23.78). But Montaigne himself can barely stand to watch someone wring the neck of a chicken (II.11.313), and while he appreciates the excitement of the hunt, he has "not been able without distress to see pursued and killed an innocent animal which is defenseless and does us no harm" (II.11.316). In one of the most remarkable passages anywhere in the *Essays*, he condemns the "imaginary kingship" that humans ascribe to themselves over nonhuman animals (II.11.318). "There is a certain respect," he says, "and a general duty of humanity, that attaches us not only to animals, who have life and feeling, but even to trees and plants.... There is some relationship between them and us, and some mutual obligation" (II.11.318). Four and a half centuries after these words were written, people who have never read Montaigne insist on the truth of the ideas they convey.

It is important to acknowledge that Montaigne is not altogether ahead of his time in despising cruelty. The Dominican cleric Bartolomé de Las Casas, for instance, published his *Short Account of the Destruction of the Indies* in 1552—a book that denounced the many acts of violence committed against Native Americans by Spanish officials and landowners during the early decades of New World colonization. Nor does Montaigne oppose capital punishment, though he is adamant that "all that goes beyond plain death seems to me pure cruelty, especially for us who ought to have some concern about sending souls away in a good state" (II.11.314). Rather, Montaigne's sense of the interconnectedness of life forms, human and otherwise, stands out as truly extraordinary. And while the suggestion that an ethical imperative against cruelty might be entailed by such interconnectedness could not have held the power in 1580 that it holds today, one suspects that even in the sixteenth century Montaigne had readers who would have been willing to trade local for global allegiances and to reform ethical codes within a larger ecology of reference.

Mechanical victories

Montaigne's anti-ethnocentric meditations surface once again in "Of Coaches," a chapter first published in 1588. After contemplating the ostentatious displays of wealth and liberality with which he is familiar from histories of antiquity, Montaigne turns to the simplicity of that "other world" that has been known to Europeans for less than a century: a world "no less great, full, and well-limbed than [the Old], yet so new and so infantile that it is still being taught its A B C" (III.6.693). He worries that America will be sickened by the "contagion" of Europe—hastened toward decline before reaching its full maturity. And such a fate would be unspeakably tragic, for its peoples are "not at all behind us in natural brightness of mind" (III.6.693).

Even in the Old World, Montaigne was familiar with the spoliation of near-utopian locales. In "Of the Resemblance of Children to Fathers," for instance, he speaks of a place called Lahontan at the base of the Pyrenees, a secluded and tranquil district whose inhabitants had lived apart for centuries until an ambitious young man "began to disdain their ancient customs and to put into their heads the notion of the pomp of the regions on this side of the mountains" (II.37.591). But in America the destruction of long-established cultures was incalculably more extensive. Not only were native populations enslaved, forced into Christianity, and exposed to diseases to which they had no resistance; they were also subjected to hideous regimes of cruelty. Montaigne mentions one instance in which more than four hundred men were burned alive, and he writes in detail about the ghastly tortures inflicted on the kings of Peru and Mexico before their eventual deaths (III.6.696–97). Alert as well to the absurdities of colonial policy as exemplified by the *Requerimiento*—a document informing native peoples that the

pope had given their lands to the Spanish Crown—Montaigne
bitterly laments the lost opportunity for Europeans to establish "a
brotherly fellowship" with the inhabitants of America:

> So many cities razed, so many nations exterminated, so many
> millions of people put to the sword, and the richest and most beautiful
> part of the world turned upside down, for the traffic in pearls and
> pepper! Base and mechanical victories! Never did ambition, never
> did public enmities, drive men against one another to such horrible
> hostilities and such miserable calamities. (III.6.695)

Seldom vehement and never maudlin, Montaigne is nowhere
more impassioned than here.

The *Essays*' American chapters associate the New World with
Golden Age innocence, purity, and unlimited potential. Montaigne
knows that this exaggerates the truth, but he knows as well that he
gains more than he loses through such rhetorical exposition. In
particular, he secures tremendous leverage in his ongoing project
of social critique, unforgettably exposing the presumption,
brutality, and Iron Age cunning of his fellow Europeans. The
preface to his book, moreover, acquires heightened resonance
once we have read "Of Coaches" and "Of Cannibals": "Had I been
placed among these nations which are said to live still in the sweet
freedom of nature's first laws, I assure you that I should very
gladly have portrayed myself here entire and wholly naked" ("To
the Reader," 2). One might say that the *Essays*, at least in spirit,
amount to a distinctly American venture.

Montaigne's allusion to the *Requerimiento*

Prepared in 1512 by the Castilian jurist Juan López de Palacios
Rubios, the *Requerimiento* ("Requirement") was designed to
ensure legal indemnity for Spanish conquistadors as they

subjugated Native American peoples, seizing their lands and property. Clerical officials were instructed to read the document aloud to native leaders, most of whom did not understand Spanish. Here is an abridged extract from the *Requerimiento* that includes the "threats" to which Montaigne refers in his allusion to the document:

"On behalf of His Majesty [King Ferdinand II],...I beg and require you as best I can...[to] recognize the Church as lord and superior of the universal world, and the most elevated Pope...in its name, and His Majesty in his place as lord and king....His Majesty and I in his name will receive you...and leave your women and children free, without servitude, so that you can freely do what you wish...and we will not compel you to turn Christians. But if you do not do it...with the help of God, I will enter forcefully against you, and I will make war everywhere and however I can, and I will subject you to the yoke of the Church and His Majesty, and I will take your wives and children, and I will make them slaves....I will take your goods, and I will do to you all the evil that a lord may do to vassals who do not obey him. And I solemnly declare that the deaths and damages will be your fault and not that of His Majesty, nor mine, nor of the gentlemen who came with me."

"Coasting the sea in quest of their mines, certain Spaniards landed in a fertile, pleasant, well-populated country, and made their usual declarations to its people: that they were peaceable men, coming from distant voyages, sent on behalf of the king of Castile, the greatest prince of the habitable world, to whom the Pope, representing God on earth, had given principality of all the Indies; that if these people would be tributaries to him, they would be very kindly treated. They demanded of them food to eat and gold to be used in a certain medicine, and expounded to them the belief in one single God and the truth of our religion, which they advised them to accept, adding a few threats" (III.6.695).

Chapter 7
Providential diversity

"The world is nothing but variety and dissimilarity," says
Montaigne (II.2.244); "Nature has committed herself to make
nothing separate that is not different" (III.13.815). He knows that
it scarcely follows from such claims that we should ignore the
countless instances of similitude among worldly phenomena. But
he insists on pressing his point: "Resemblance does not make
things so much alike as difference makes them unalike"
(III.13.815). Montaigne's implicit question, then, is how we should
make sense of diversity. What are its forms of significance and
value? Can it be privileged over sameness, given that both
concepts derive meaning through interdependence? Is diversity
inherently unsettling? If so, why? How can we best adapt
ourselves to its apparent inevitability?

America is a prime site of alterity for Montaigne, a vast realm of
otherness from which he repeatedly summons modes of being and
doing that conflict with those of Europe. In the "Apology for
Raymond Sebond," for example, he alludes to his encounter with the
natives of Brazil, lampooning his countrymen's response:

> Because we did not understand their language at all, and because
> their ways, moreover, and their bearing and clothes were totally
> remote from ours, which of us did not attribute it to stupidity and
> brutishness to see them mute, ignorant of the French language,

ignorant of our hand-kissings and our serpentine bows, our
deportment and our bearing, which human nature must take as its
pattern without fail? Everything that seems strange to us we
condemn, and everything that we do not understand. (II.12.343)

The human tendency to interpret difference as inferiority is one of
Montaigne's great quarries, a phenomenon he challenges in all
strata of the *Essays*. Most people, he argues, relegate unfamiliar
forms of behavior and thought to the categories of the improper, the
unnatural, and the barbaric. As he notes in a late addition to his
chapter on Seneca and Plutarch, "it seems to each man that the
ruling pattern of nature is in him; to this he refers all other forms
as a touchstone. The ways that do not square with his are counterfeit
and artificial. What brutish stupidity!" (II.32.548). To be sure,
Montaigne's view softens at times; he acknowledges that "it is a
common vice, not of the vulgar only but of almost all men, to fix their
aim and limit by the ways to which they were born" (I.49.215). But
he himself has avoided this vice—or so he says—and it is evident that
he would much prefer that people avail themselves of an unbiased
consideration of all things that strike them as abnormal or alien.

If the unfamiliar can be drawn within the bounds of open-minded
assessment, the familiar can likewise be estranged. Montaigne
provides a vivid example in his chapter "Of Custom." A gentleman
he once knew had the habit of blowing his nose in his hand rather
than in a handkerchief. Not surprisingly, people found this
disgusting. But the man asked Montaigne "what privilege this
dirty excrement has that we should prepare a fine delicate piece of
linen to receive it, and then, what's more, to wrap it up and carry
it"—and Montaigne conceded that what the man said was "not
entirely without reason" (I.23.80). He recognized, in short, that
his own habituation to cultural norms had prevented him from
perceiving the strangeness of a common European practice.

And this is one of Montaigne's unifying claims throughout his
treatment of the customary and the familiar. Not only does

habituation dull our judgment and stifle our curiosity: it diminishes our freedom of thought. The principal effect of custom, he writes, is to "ensnare us in such a way that it is hardly within our power to get ourselves out of its grip and return into ourselves to reflect and reason about its ordinances" (I.23.83). Many people—perhaps most—are disabled by custom's narcotic influence. But Montaigne is confident that recovering our faculties of discernment is always possible, provided that we make a conscious, concerted effort to withdraw ourselves from the onslaught of conventional opinion; we must refer our thoughts instead to the standards of "truth and reason" (I.23.85). Whether truth and reason are as readily accessible as Montaigne implies is a matter to which we will return. What is indisputable, however, is that custom's tyranny is a perennial feature of human social existence, and for Montaigne it contributes enormously to the ubiquitous but misguided view that "whatever is not as we are is worth nothing" (II.12.358).

Monsters, miracles, and belief

But how do questions of habituation shift or evolve when we leave the secular sphere and move to the realms of conviction and belief? This is an issue that Montaigne raises on multiple occasions and in varied contexts, not only in the "Apology" but also in such chapters as "Of a Monstrous Child," "Of Cripples," and "It Is Folly to Measure the True and False by Our Own Capacity." In the latter essay, Montaigne begins by noting that if we think of belief as an impression made on the mind, it is not surprising that ease of conviction is most frequently observed among the young, the infirm, and the uneducated, since their minds are not sufficiently ballasted with matter and force to resist imprinting from without (I.27.132). But Montaigne quickly complicates this analysis. "It is foolish presumption," he writes, "to go around disdaining and condemning as false whatever does not seem likely to us" (I.27.132). The opposition he thus establishes lies between an uncritical readiness to believe and a critical complacency that mocks such belief. He admits that he has at times been guilty of the latter tendency, but "reason" has taught him that "to condemn a thing, dogmatically, as false and impossible, is to assume the advantage of knowing the bounds and limits of God's will and of the power of our mother Nature" (I.27.132). It is both absurd and dangerous, he says, to presume that we can judge "the limits of possibility" (I.27.133).

This is not to suggest that we should revert to childlike ease of belief. But at the very least we should keep our human fallibility constantly in mind and discipline ourselves against premature dismissal of that which strikes us as unlikely. Take miracles, for instance. Saint Augustine describes many miracles that he witnessed firsthand; shall we therefore accuse him of credulity— or, worse, of imposture (I.27.134)? If we find it hard to accept such claims even from a great saint, we should at least "leave in suspense" those allegations to which we cannot extend belief (I.27.133). Indeed, Montaigne returns to this position from a very different angle in his Book Three chapter "Of Cripples." Discussing the zeal with which a certain prince sought to persuade him of the reality of witchcraft, Montaigne notes that after interviewing several "witches" himself, he thinks it more appropriate to give them hellebore than hemlock, which is to say that he finds them mentally ill rather than criminally malevolent. Citing Augustine again, he adds that "it is better to lean toward doubt than toward assurance in things difficult to prove and dangerous to believe" (III.11.789–90).

Presumption, then, can work in multiple ways, allowing us to dismiss what seems improbable as well as to act on inadequate evidence. The common denominator would seem to be hubris: an overconfidence in one's powers of judgment combined with a persistent lack of humility. For Montaigne, presumption is "our natural and original malady," the anthropocentric trait that allows us to deem ourselves superior to all other creatures despite our inhabitation of "the worst, deadest, and most stagnant part of the universe, on the lowest story of the house and the farthest from the vault of heaven" (II.12.330-31). Consider the way we talk about monstrosity. Raising this issue in "Of a Monstrous Child," Montaigne describes a pair of conjoined twins he has recently seen, one of whom was born without a head. Montaigne's implication is that this unfortunate being, just fourteen months old, is regarded as a "monster" by all those who view him. But the essayist challenges this interpretation by foregrounding human ignorance: "What we call monsters are not so to God, who sees in the immensity of his work the infinity of forms that he has comprised within it" (II.30.539). It is an act of gross presumption to label as monstrous that which is merely unfamiliar. As Montaigne observes in "Of Coaches," "If we saw as much of the world as we do not see, we would perceive, it is likely, a perpetual multiplication and vicissitude of forms. There is nothing unique and rare as regards nature, but there certainly is as regards our knowledge, which is a miserable foundation for our rules and which is apt to represent to us a very false picture of things" (III.6.693). By this logic, neither the "monstrous child" nor the native peoples of America are any less natural than the pedigreed aristocrats of Europe.

In essence, Montaigne's argument is that whatever we term monstrous or miraculous must be reassessed from the perspective of human finitude. "We must not judge what is possible, and what is not, according to what is credible and incredible to our sense" (II.32.548). The realm of the natural far exceeds any human ability to perceive or understand it; most of what exists is unknown to us. Embracing the Protagorean dictum that "man is the measure of all things" is thus ludicrously inadequate as a response to worldly diversity. The terms *monster* and *miracle* should never be unthinkingly aligned with the category of the unnatural. Whatever else they may denote, first and foremost they signify our inescapable deficiencies of comprehension.

Conformity and divine providence

Montaigne loves diversity. He believes that it possesses inherent pedagogical value, and he also suggests that it can be conducive to happiness: "The diversity in fashions from one nation to another affects me only with the pleasure of variety.... I have encountered hardly any customs that are not as good as ours" (III.9.753–54). Montaigne also enjoys estranging the familiar—and he is exceptionally good at doing so. Contemplating what we now call genetic inheritance, he marvels at the notion that a drop of semen can carry "the impressions not only of the bodily form but of the thoughts and inclinations of our fathers!" (II.37.578). And in "Of Cripples," after acknowledging that "we become habituated to anything strange by use and time," he seizes on the fact that his long-sustained project of self-writing has led to an unexpected and paradoxical result: "the more I frequent myself and know myself, the more my deformity astonishes me, and the less I understand myself" (III.11.787). In this case, the familiar and the strange have become indistinguishable.

On occasion, and for the most part in post-1580 developments of the *Essays*, Montaigne allows his ruminations to lead him toward conclusions that are as scathingly critical of his contemporaries as those we have encountered in "Of Cannibals" and "Of Coaches." Complaining in the "Apology," for instance, about the accidental and unreflective ways in which people often reach their religious convictions, he writes that "another region, other witnesses, similar promises and threats, might imprint upon us in the same way a contrary belief. We are Christians by the same title that we are Perigordians or Germans" (II.12.325). Likewise, in "Of Experience," while discussing legal codes and statutes, he claims that "laws remain in credit not because they are just, but because they are laws. That is the mystic foundation of their authority" (III.13.821). And in "Of Custom" he goes so far as to declare that "the laws of conscience, which we say are born of nature, are born of custom" (I.23.83)—a statement that, if true, carries the potential of profoundly unsettling us with regard to the wisdom of our own practices. Montaigne is clearly troubled by the arbitrariness and lack of intellectual rigor with which people routinely approach ethical, legal, and religious questions, so it is perhaps unsurprising that he resorts at times to pronouncements such as these—pronouncements readily susceptible to being quoted out of context or highlighted without attention to their irony or hyperbole.

But for all the problems engendered by custom and habituation, Montaigne finally argues that in our public lives we should conform to the established ways of our region and country. "Society has no right to our thoughts," he says; "but the rest—our actions, our work, our fortunes, our very life—we must lend and abandon to its service and to the common opinions....It is the rule of rules, and the universal law of laws, that each man should observe those of the place he is in" (I.23.86). Even La Boétie, who according to Montaigne was at heart a republican rather than a monarchist, bore the following precept engraved "on his soul": "to obey and submit most religiously to the laws under which he was born" (I.28.144).

Strong precedent for such a view may be found within the synoptic gospels and Pauline epistles. As Jesus says to the Pharisees in the Gospel of Matthew, "Give unto Caesar that which is Caesar's, and unto God that which is God's." Montaigne is clearly aware of this precedent; he praises Christianity's insistence on obedience to secular authority as one of its marks of "utmost justice" (I.23.87–88). But his subscription to social conformity does not derive solely from Christian faith. His study of the Hellenistic philosophical schools, among them the Epicureans and the Pyrrhonian skeptics, has taught him that even the least conventional sects submit to local law (II.12.374–80). More importantly, his admiration of Socrates grounds his belief in civil compliance. If a man of this caliber "refused to save his life by disobedience to the magistrate" (I.23.86), how can humans of incomparably lesser integrity justify insubordination? Only in the most extreme circumstances does Montaigne sanction the abandonment of social and legal precedent. In such cases, he says, "it would be better to make the laws will what they can do, since they cannot do what they will" (I.23.89). But these are rare and aberrant occasions. Montaigne's implication is that as soon as political stability has been reestablished, civil obedience once again becomes the tacit duty of every citizen.

Above all else, Montaigne's endorsement of conformity is linked to a conception of providence as the force that finally resolves the problems posed by diversity of belief. This is most readily apparent in the "Apology," though it is implicit in several other chapters. Montaigne almost never uses the word *providence*, but to the extent that he understands himself to be placed by God in a certain part of the world at a certain moment in history, he trusts that his own inadequacy in choosing among multiple opinions constitutes a reason "to accept other people's choice and stay in the position where God put me" (II.12.428). In other words, it would be presumptuous of him to deem himself capable of assessing the comparative truth value of the complex devotional and theological views to which he has been exposed. After spending several pages, for instance, rehearsing ancient opinions on the nature of divinity, he concludes that "the confusion in the ways of the world has gained this from me, that conduct and fancies different from mine do not so much displease me as instruct me, do not so much swell my pride as humble me when I compare them; and any choice other than that which comes from the hand of God seems to me a choice of little advantage" (II.12.383).

We might well ask how Montaigne can know that a particular choice derives from God's hand. But setting this aside as an unanswerable question, it is clear from his reasoning that he regards diversity of belief and worship as providential, for it can humble us and open us to divine direction. And thus, in

8. The chapel on the ground level of Montaigne's tower; the essayist would have often attended Catholic Mass in this room.

contemplating the implication of the Greek god Apollo that ancient religions were purely human inventions, he is led to the following exclamation: "O God, what an obligation do we not have to the benignity of our sovereign creator for having freed our belief from the folly of those vagabond and arbitrary devotions, and having based it on the eternal foundation of his holy word!" (II.12.436–37). Scripture does not figure largely within the *Essays*, but it is nonetheless identified by Montaigne as the criterion by means of which final judgments regarding the diversity of religious thought may be proffered.

The world, for Montaigne, is incorrigibly plural. He would have it no other way. And his ruminations on diversity, scattered through many chapters, lead to a remarkable constellation of insights and emphases. "I do not share that common error of judging another by myself," he writes; "I believe in and conceive a thousand contrary ways of life, and in contrast with the common run of men, I more easily admit difference than resemblance between us"

(I.37.169). As an element, perhaps, of his "ruling pattern" (III.2.615), this tendency aids Montaigne in his study of custom and habituation, helping him describe the conceptual distortions they routinely encourage. But while he welcomes the strange and repeatedly estranges the familiar, he also urges us to accept the laws and practices of our region, acknowledging their inevitable imperfection. "The oldest and best-known evil is always more bearable than an evil that is new and untried" (III.9.732). Such acceptance, however, is quite distinct from belief in the truth or permanent rightness of these practices. Belief of the latter sort is limited to the spiritual guidance provided through revealed knowledge. We are unimaginably fortunate, according to Montaigne, to have been granted the book of Scripture; but divine providence is likewise evident in that other book—the book of Nature—whose endless display of rival means of ordering human experience can also steer us toward truths immune to doubt.

Chapter 8
Skepticism

No characterization of Montaigne has held greater sway than that
he is a skeptic: an arch-practitioner of philosophical skepticism as
well as a man who is skeptically minded by nature. Pascal and
Emerson saw him this way, as have countless other readers from
the seventeenth century to the present. But what does such a
characterization mean? And how can it coexist with what we
know of Montaigne's devotional identity—his Roman Catholic
faith and practice? These and similar questions shape the
following discussion. Montaigne, it may be argued, is skeptical in
two distinct fashions. On the one hand, he sometimes exhibits a
moderately rigorous epistemological skepticism that is clearly
informed by wide reading in ancient sources. But on the other, he
frequently displays a looser, more general, and less doctrinaire
skepticism that seems intimately tied to his own temperament
and intellectual disposition. These skepticisms are related, and at
times they overlap, but they are best treated separately so that
their origins and key features may be sharply distinguished.

Pyrrhonian skepticism and the doubt of the later Academy

Midway through the "Apology for Raymond Sebond," Montaigne
summarizes the taxonomy of major philosophical outlooks offered
by the Hellenistic skeptic Sextus Empiricus. "Whoever seeks

anything," he writes, "comes to this point: he says either that he has found it, or that it cannot be found, or that he is still in quest of it. All philosophy is divided into these three types" (II.12.371). The first type, in Sextus's opinion, is exemplified by Aristotelians, Epicureans, Stoics, and other thinkers who are confident not only that knowledge may be obtained but that they have obtained a great deal of it. Without denigration, he describes such thinkers as "dogmatic." Montaigne follows suit, but with pejorative overtones: Aristotle, for instance, is "the prince of dogmatists" (II.12.376). For our purposes here, and to distinguish between varieties of dogmatism, we will refer to philosophers of this kind as "positive dogmatists": positive in the sense that they believe the human mind is capable of reaching truth and of formulating any number of valid truth claims. Monotheism, polytheism, and atheism, according to this view, are all examples of positive dogmatism.

The second type—those who assert that truth cannot be found— are primarily exemplified by philosophers of the later Platonic Academy. In particular, Montaigne mentions Carneades and his disciple Clitomachus, both of whom served as leaders of the Academy during the second century BCE. What unites these thinkers, from Montaigne's perspective, is that they endorse the concept of *acatalepsia*: the view that while truth may ultimately exist, it cannot be apprehended by reason or sense perception. "The conclusion of these men," says Montaigne, is that we are beset by a deep and inescapable ignorance (II.12.371); we should therefore abandon the quest for certainty and content ourselves with inductively derived probabilities. But in their "conclusion" that the acquisition of knowledge is impossible, these philosophers are in fact dogmatic, if only with respect to a single proposition. As a consequence, we will refer to them here as "negative dogmatists." Montaigne does not use this term, but he suggests its pertinence when he writes that there exists "an overbold vanity in that second class [of philosophers] who assure us that human powers are not capable of attaining truth" (II.12.371, III.11.792).

Sextus Empiricus on Pyrrhonian skepticism

"When people are investigating any subject, the likely result is either a discovery, a denial of discovery and a confession of inapprehensibility, or else a continuation of the investigation. This, no doubt, is why in the case of philosophical investigations, some have said that they have discovered the truth, some have asserted that it cannot be apprehended, and others are still investigating.... Those who are called Dogmatists think that they have discovered the truth—for example, the schools of Aristotle, Epicurus, the Stoics, and others. The schools of Clitomachus, Carneades, and other Academics, have asserted that things cannot be apprehended. And the sceptics are still investigating. Hence the most fundamental kinds of philosophy are thought to be three: the Dogmatic, the Academic, and the Sceptical.... The Sceptical persuasion is also called Investigative [*zetetic*], from its activity in investigating and inquiring; Suspensive, from the feeling that comes about in the inquirer after the investigation; Aporetic, either from the fact that it puzzles over and investigates everything or else from its being at a loss whether to assent or deny; and Pyrrhonian, from the fact that Pyrrho appears to have attached himself to Scepticism more systematically and conspicuously than anyone before him.... Scepticism is an ability to set out oppositions among things which appear and are thought of in any way at all, an ability by which, because of the equipollence [*isostheneia*, i.e., equal persuasiveness] in the opposed objects and accounts, we come first to suspension of judgement [*epochē*] and afterwards to tranquillity [*ataraxia*]" (Sextus Empiricus, *Outlines of Pyrrhonism*, ca. 200 CE).

The third type are the skeptics. More precisely, they are Pyrrhonian skeptics: followers of the Greek philosopher Pyrrho, a younger contemporary of Aristotle in the late fourth and early third centuries BCE. The basic intellectual activity of the

Pyrrhonists, according to Montaigne, "is to waver, doubt, and search, to be sure of nothing, to answer for nothing"; "they use their reason to inquire and debate, but not to conclude and choose" (II.12.372, II.12.374). As "the wisest school of philosophers," they find that "there is no reason that does not have its opposite" (II.15.463), so they pile up claims and counterclaims, examining all of them but suspending judgment with regard to their truth value. This judgmental suspension (*epochē*) leads them in turn to *ataraxia*: "a peaceful and sedate condition of life, exempt from the agitations we receive through the impression of the opinion and knowledge we think we have of things" (II.12.372). Pyrrhonism, then, is a form of epistemological skepticism motivated by a desire for emotional and cerebral tranquility. Fundamentally therapeutic in nature, it is distinctively characterized by its agnostic outlook regarding claims to knowledge and truth.

Most scholars believe that Montaigne read Sextus Empiricus's *Outlines of Pyrrhonism* during the mid-1570s, three or four years after he began drafting his *Essays*. The book, written in Greek around 200 CE, had been translated into Latin and published in 1562, so Sextus's account of skepticism was readily available to an accomplished Latinist such as Montaigne. This translation also included a brief biography of Pyrrho by Diogenes Laertius, a historian of philosophy who wrote during the third century CE. Montaigne's copy of Sextus has not survived, but because the essayist repeatedly paraphrases material from the *Outlines*, particularly in his "Apology," it is evident that he knew the book well. He had also been exposed to a critique of Pyrrhonism that appears in Lucretius's lengthy poem *On the Nature of Things*. Montaigne's copy of this poem is still extant, and the text is heavily annotated in his hand; he clearly read it with sustained intensity.

In addition to Pyrrhonism, however, Montaigne was also familiar with the skepticism of the Platonic Academy. He alludes to Carneades and Clitomachus in his "Apology," and while these figures are occasionally mentioned in Sextus's *Outlines*, their views are presented in much greater detail in Cicero's *Academics*, two dialogues on the nature and possibility of knowledge that were widely read in European humanist circles from the fifteenth century forward. Never a great admirer of Cicero, Montaigne nonetheless knew many of his works: he quotes frequently from *The Nature of the Gods* and *The Tusculan Disputations* as well as from the *Academics*, particularly in post-1588 additions to the *Essays*. Thus, between the writings of Sextus, Cicero, Lucretius, and Diogenes Laertius, Montaigne had read most of the extant accounts of ancient skepticism. He was as well positioned as anyone in sixteenth-century Europe to incorporate opinions shaped by these accounts within his own discussions of topics in which epistemological considerations are centrally important.

The most crucial discussion of this sort appears in the "Apology for Raymond Sebond." As we know, Pierre Eyquem asked his son to translate Sebond's *Natural Theology* from Latin into French; Montaigne did so and published the work in 1569. The Vatican, however, had placed Sebond's treatise on its *Index of Prohibited Books* a decade earlier, largely owing to the author's extremely optimistic assessment of human reason. For Sebond, the truths proffered by the book of Scripture—the Judeo-Christian Bible—are fully corroborated by the book of Nature, or the world of God's creation, where humans make use of the innate capacities with which they have been endowed. Contemplating the natural world by means of their rational faculties enables them, according to Sebond, to confirm the existence of an omnipotent Creator, along with the truth of the central doctrines of Christianity. But from the Vatican's perspective, at least in the late 1550s, such claims conferred an unacceptably high level of confidence upon the efficacy of ratiocination. Still, in 1564, when a revised version of the *Index* appeared, only the prologue of Sebond's book remained censored, and indeed this is where his optimism had been most vehemently expressed. Probably unaware of the Vatican's concerns, Montaigne nonetheless tempered the Spaniard's extravagance in his rendition of the prologue. And this seems to have been effective: his translation of the *Natural Theology* was never placed on the *Index*.

But Montaigne had reservations of his own. While Sebond's arguments were regarded as a potent rebuttal of atheism as well as a useful antidote to the attractions of Protestant thought, they also ran the risk of obviating the very need for faith among Christian believers. Alert to this problem, and deeply skeptical about Sebond's praise of reason, Montaigne found himself in an awkward position as he prepared his "apology" for Sebond's treatise—a task imposed on him by Marguerite de Valois, wife of Henri de Navarre and sister to King Henri III. He concedes, for instance, that the *Natural Theology* is a "rich and splendid" work (II.12.320), but his defense of the treatise relies heavily on the premise that Sebond's critics are no more persuasive than is Sebond himself. Aware that this is a "desperate" tactic (II.12.419), Montaigne insists nonetheless that those who attack Sebond's claims are more notable for their presumption than for their wisdom or intellectual temperance:

> The means I take to beat down this frenzy, and which seems fittest to me, is to crush and trample underfoot human arrogance and pride; to make them feel the inanity, the vanity and nothingness, of man; to wrest from their hands the puny weapons of their reason; to make them bow their heads and bite the ground beneath the authority and reverence of divine majesty. (II.12.327)

And it is at this point in the "Apology" that Montaigne begins a lengthy disquisition on the frailty and imperfection of all human beings. He argues that in many respects we are inferior to nonhuman animals; he claims that knowledge can make us neither good nor happy; indeed he questions whether we can acquire knowledge at all. What do we know of God, for example? What do we know of the soul? Can we trust the conclusions we reach through laborious acts of reasoning? Can we even trust the impressions yielded by our senses—the impressions of sight, sound, smell, touch, and taste? Is it possible that we are dreaming when we think we are awake—or that our conscious existence is "another kind of sleep?" (II.12.451). Treating such matters in detail, and quoting from an enormous range of sources, Montaigne seeks to undermine the confidence displayed not only by Sebond's critics but by all those who might be viewed as positive dogmatists in their reliance on reason as a basis for the advancement of truth claims. Reason, after all, is "a touchstone full of falsity, error, weakness, and impotence" (II.12.405); it "does nothing but go astray in everything, especially when it meddles with divine things" (II.12.386). And this leads to Montaigne's concluding argument. Even if we are capable of acquiring knowledge through our own capacities—a highly dubious prospect—such knowledge is mere vanity unless it is infused with divine grace. As Montaigne asserts at the end of his chapter, humanity is incapable of rising above its inherent limitations: "[Man] will rise," he says, only "by abandoning and renouncing his own means, and letting himself be raised and uplifted by purely celestial means" (II.12.457).

Pyrrhonian epistemology

Before making this pronouncement, however, Montaigne dwells on several key features of Pyrrhonian thought as he presents his case for human inadequacy. He acknowledges, for instance, that language itself poses a problem for Pyrrhonists inasmuch as it relies heavily on declarative modes of expression. To communicate their ideas with the utmost lucidity, Pyrrhonian skeptics "need a new language," since languages such as Latin and French are "wholly formed of affirmative propositions" (II.12.392). While this is not in fact true, Montaigne's point is that when skeptics say "I doubt," their opponents are immediately enabled to accuse them of being certain about this very matter: that they doubt. As a consequence, Pyrrhonists have been forced to stipulate that when they resort to affirmative claims, their claims extinguish themselves at the precise moment of articulation. Montaigne supplies a useful metaphor: Pyrrhonian propositions are like rhubarb, "which expels evil humors and carries itself off with them" (II.12.393). Even more helpfully, he suggests that the outlook of the skeptics is most accurately conveyed "in the form of interrogation: 'What do I know?'" (II.12.393). Sextus Empiricus would have been delighted.

Montaigne also attends to issues of sense perception. He wonders, among other things, whether humans are equipped "with all the senses of nature. I see many animals that live a complete and perfect life, some without sight, others without hearing; who knows whether we too do not still lack one, two, three, or many other senses?" (II.12.444). More crucially, he grapples with what is known among theorists of knowledge as "the problem of the criterion." Recognizing that sense perception is notoriously inaccurate, that it can be affected by the age, health, or mood of the perceiver, and that we can always doubt whether what we perceive is reliably representative of the supposed object of perception, Montaigne asks how we should ascertain the truth or falsity of conflicting perceptual appearances. "To judge the appearances that we receive of objects," he says, "we need a judicatory instrument; to verify this instrument, we need a demonstration; to verify the demonstration, an instrument: and there we are in a circle" (II.12.454). He is conscious, in short, that for accurate judgment we require a *criterion* of judgment, but that before we can know that our criterion is valid, we must already know what is accurate. Otherwise our criterion will be unconvincing. Some philosophers would disagree with the imputation of circularity that Sextus and Montaigne ascribe to the criterion problem, but this is of small consequence here; the upshot for Montaigne is that while we can describe the appearances that sense perception yields, we cannot be certain that they constitute truthful impressions of objects in the outside world. And from this point it is only a short step to external-world skepticism, or doubt about whether anything exists apart from the mind of the perceiving subject. Montaigne does not take this step. But half a century later, one of his most brilliant readers, René Descartes, contemplates precisely such questions.

Finally, Montaigne wrestles with the distinctions between Academic and Pyrrhonian skepticism. From his reading of Sextus and Cicero he is aware of the differences attributed to these schools, and when it suits him he can marshal relevant arguments for specific issues—usually to the detriment of the Academics. He reminds us, for instance, that while these philosophers "affirmed that we are not capable of knowing, and that truth is engulfed in deep abysses where human sight cannot penetrate, they still admitted that some things are more probable than others." Yet he immediately proceeds to assault the case for probabilism:

> How can they let themselves be inclined toward the likeness of truth, if they know not the truth? How do they know the semblance of that whose essence they do not know? Either we can judge absolutely, or we absolutely cannot. (II.12.422)

The Academics are always negative dogmatists from Montaigne's point of view, and such an orientation is inevitably tainted by hubris. But Montaigne is fully prepared to acknowledge commonalities between Pyrrhonian and Academic skepticism when doing so serves to combat dogmatism of the positive variety. Taking issue with the Epicurean view that sense perception is inherently reliable, he notes that "the schools that dispute man's knowledge dispute it principally because of the uncertainty and weakness of our senses" (II.12.446). And using sixteenth-century medical practice as a prime example of the limitations of human knowledge, he concludes that "thence came that ancient opinion of the philosophers who located the sovereign good in the recognition of the weakness of our judgment" (II.12.362). This conflation of the Academic and Pyrrhonian schools shows that Montaigne is sometimes more drawn to the broad, unifying characteristics of skeptical thought than to differences among

9. Montaigne arranged for more than fifty passages from classical literature and the Bible to be inscribed on the rafters of his library, on the third floor of his tower, including sentences and keywords from Sextus Empiricus.

competing groups. And he is never a systematic philosopher; to be so would be to succumb to the very presumption against which he so often rails. The affinities between the followers of Pyrrho and Socrates can be just as significant as the points of contention. "Of three general sects of philosophy," after all, "two make express profession of doubt and ignorance" (II.12.375).

Montaignian skepticism

Doubt and ignorance unquestionably rank among the most vital features of Montaigne's outlook on the world. His ideal teacher exposes students to multiple perspectives rather than dictating what they should believe. Similar views appear throughout the *Essays*—and in all compositional strata. Montaigne opens the early chapter "Of the Uncertainty of Our Judgment" by noting that "there is much to be said on all matters, both for and against" (I.47.205), and in a late addition to the "Apology" he stresses that dogmatism amounts to a mindset "by which we are not allowed *not* to know what we do not know" (II.12.373). There is in fact "a certain strong and generous ignorance that concedes nothing to knowledge in honor and courage, an ignorance that requires no less knowledge to conceive than does knowledge itself" (III.11.788).

In short, Montaigne experiences no discomfort in entertaining doubt or confessing ignorance. He claims in "Of Democritus and Heraclitus" that ignorance is his "ruling quality" (I.50.219), and in "Of Cripples" he goes so far as to say that "all the abuses of this world are engendered by our being taught to be afraid of professing our ignorance and our being bound to accept everything that we cannot refute" (III.11.788). For Montaigne, suspending judgment on complicated matters is never a bad idea, and assenting promptly to the views of others is seldom a good one. Judgmental suspension, moreover, can be extended "as much in the direction of rejecting as of accepting" (III.11.788). Take the practice of divination. If we suspend judgment regarding the validity of this practice, we avoid the gullibility associated with uncritical acceptance. But if we suspend judgment regarding the wholesale rejection of its claims, we tacitly acknowledge the limitations of our own understanding. Montaigne sees value in both forms of doubt. He would surely have agreed with Shakespeare's Hamlet that "there are more things in heaven and earth than are dreamt of in our philosophy."

What we might call "Montaignian skepticism" is thus a pragmatic and case-oriented synthesis of doubt, inquiry, and provisional conclusion. It embraces ignorance, it valorizes detached investigation, and it prizes humility and self-critique, but it also assumes that certain truths exist. It is acutely sensitive to linguistic nuance, as when Montaigne tells us that "I love those words which soften and moderate the rashness of our propositions: 'perhaps,' 'to some extent,' 'some,' 'they say,' 'I think,' and the like" (III.11.788). At times it takes the form of relativism, and Montaigne is justly famous for imagining the world from a feline perspective: "When I play with my cat, who knows if I am not a pastime to her more than she is to me?" (II.12.331). And it has a particularly vexed relationship with the power of authority. Montaigne is sharply critical of people who accept opinions, customs, and beliefs without examining them or juxtaposing them against other modes of thought or behavior, yet he himself might be arraigned on precisely these grounds—above all in matters of faith. As we know, late in the "Apology" he makes the following vehement claim: "what an obligation do we not have to the benignity of our sovereign creator . . . for having based [our belief] on the eternal foundation of his holy word!" (II.12.436–37). Sextus Empiricus would never have countenanced such an exclamation; he would have urged Montaigne to submit the truth claims of Christianity to the same judgmental suspension reserved for other dogmatic assertions. But Montaigne cannot sustain Pyrrhonian analysis to this degree. Like most Europeans of his time, he understands Scripture as holding an ontological status both prior to and utterly distinct from that of custom, law, and statecraft. "The things that come to us from heaven," he says, "have alone the right and authority for persuasion, alone the stamp of truth; which also we do not see with our own eyes, or receive by our own means" (II.12.423).

One might be curious as to how we can ascertain that something has "come to us from heaven." But this is a question not to be asked. Many of Montaigne's readers, unsurprisingly, have wondered whether he could possibly be sincere in his professions of Christian faith when he is so exceptionally capable of extending doubt in all other directions. Such wonder, however, imposes a post-Enlightenment perspective on a pre-Enlightenment phenomenon, and it also ignores the considerable evidence we have regarding Montaigne's devotional life. We know, for instance, that he routinely attended Mass—his *Travel Journal* attests to this repeatedly—and that he claimed that the Lord's Prayer had been "dictated to us word for word by the mouth of God" (I.56.229). Just as fundamentally, we know that he despised lying and deception; he wanted people to know him for who he was and never to mistake him for someone else. To misrepresent his Christian convictions would be to promote confusion about this very matter, and a man who is "hungry" to make himself known would presumably be the last person to do such a thing (III.5.643).

Most crucially, there is the issue of skepticism's social quietism. Montaigne is generally conservative with respect to programs of social or political change, and the same is true with religious observance. Here again he has the support of Academic as well as Pyrrhonian thought. Sextus stresses that skeptics live "in accordance with" the everyday practices of their culture, though he is careful to add that they hold no opinions about these practices. And Cicero, in *The Nature of the Gods*, allows his spokesman for Academic skepticism, Gaius Cotta, to expound his epistemological views in detail while simultaneously noting that he abides by "the beliefs about the immortal gods which we have inherited from our ancestors, together with our sacrifices, ceremonies, and religious observances." In acknowledging his acceptance of Roman polytheism, Cotta goes well beyond the attitude of living "in accordance with" outlined by Sextus, and indeed he informs Quintus Balbus (a stalwart Stoic) that he *believes* these gods exist—though not because the Stoics say they do. In short, Montaigne's partial conflation of Academic and Pyrrhonian skepticism facilitates the representation of his own Christian belief as an instance of social conformity within the broader skeptical tradition.

But to say this alone would be to mislead through omission. While it is true that Montaigne introduces Christianity more than once in specifically skeptical contexts (e.g., II.12.375, II.12.383–87), he does so as well when skepticism is not centrally at issue, for instance in chapters such as "Of Prayers," "Of Vain Subtleties," "Of

Freedom of Conscience," and "We Should Meddle Soberly with Judging Divine Ordinances." Montaigne's inability to view Christian truth claims in the way that Sextus would have viewed Greco-Roman religious dogma cannot be attributed solely to his familiarity with the quietism of ancient skeptical practice. This is a man, after all, who kissed the pope's foot at the Vatican (*Travel Journal*, 938–40), who left a votive offering at the Shrine of Our Lady of Loreto (*Travel Journal*, 971), and who wrote that it would be "execrable" if anything he said were deemed "against the holy prescriptions of the Catholic, Apostolic, and Roman Church, in which I die and in which I was born" (I.56.229). The nineteenth-century French critic Sainte-Beuve, who generally admired Montaigne, cautions us in *Port-Royal* that we should never mistake the essayist's apparently devout Catholicism for authentic Christian piety. But while this view may be seductive, to accept it is to cast doubt on Montaigne's entire project in the *Essays*. Our default assumption must necessarily be that Montaigne understands himself as a faithful adherent of "the old religion" (II.19.506) and that the articles of belief associated with this adherence are not susceptible to skeptical interrogation. Indeed, Montaigne would have been quite prepared to imagine that what seems blatantly contradictory from the perspective of one culture might seem fully self-consistent within another.

But Montaigne's Christianity does not blind him to Christian misbehavior. He famously notes in a late addition to the "Apology" that "there is no hostility that excels Christian hostility; our zeal does wonders when it seconds our leaning toward hatred, cruelty, ambition, avarice, detraction, rebellion" (II.12.324). Accepting the truth of a metaphysical system does not entail accepting without question the actions of that system's disciples, and this is where Montaigne's tendencies toward doubt and ignorance surface once again. They are perhaps best expressed in "Of Cripples," a chapter composed about a decade after Montaigne's most intense engagement with the skepticism of antiquity. Montaigne argues in this chapter that "it is better to lean toward doubt than toward assurance in things difficult to prove and dangerous to believe" (III.11.789–90). Having spoken with people who harbor zealous desires to prosecute witchcraft, heresy, and other ostensible transgressions, Montaigne cautions us that "to kill men, we should have sharp and luminous evidence; . . . it is putting a very high price on one's conjectures to have a man roasted alive because of them" (III.11.789–90). To say this is to set aside epistemological subtleties so as to bring Montaignian skepticism directly to bear on the most pressing issues of the era.

Skepticism, essaying, and liberty

Idiosyncratic, self-indulgent, unsystematic, incoherent: these are a few of the descriptors that might be applied to the skepticism that permeates the *Essays*. But as with other criticisms of Montaigne's book, this one would have left its author unfazed. "If I play the fool, it is at my expense and without harm to anyone; it is a folly that will die with me, and have no consequences" (II.6.273). Montaignian skepticism is a synthesis of the highly personal and the culturally authoritative; it is an eclectic hybrid, activated and valued for its utility in combating intolerance, zeal, closed-mindedness, and dogmatic assertion. But there is one final dimension of this skepticism on which we have not yet touched—a feature that more than any other links it with the larger purposes of Montaigne's enterprise.

Revising his chapter "Of Moderation" near the end of his life, Montaigne alludes to the moment in Plato's *Gorgias* when Callicles argues that philosophical investigation can be dangerous if pursued immoderately. "He speaks truly," says Montaigne, "for in its excess [philosophy] enslaves our natural freedom and, by importunate subtlety, leads us astray from the fine and level road that nature has traced for us" (I.30.146). The same might be said of any pursuit, or indeed of any kind of conviction. And the unquestioning deference to authority that Montaigne finds so problematic is perhaps best illustrated in those realms where positive dogmatism has taken firmest hold. Aristotelianism, for instance, exercises a "tyranny over our beliefs" inasmuch as it bridles "the liberty of our judgments" (II.12.403). Montaigne assumes, then, that as humans we possess an inherent freedom of thought, but that this freedom can dwindle, or vanish altogether, when we become overzealous—too devoted to a cause, too committed to a particular description of reality.

Pyrrhonian skeptics, however, retain their freedom of thought precisely by eschewing such commitment. Or so Montaigne insists. If Stoics and Epicureans wish to bind themselves to exclusive doctrines, why should skeptics not be allowed "to maintain their liberty, and to consider things without obligation and servitude?" (II.12.373). "Is it not an advantage," he continues, "to be freed from the necessity that curbs others? Is it not better to remain in suspense than to entangle yourself in the many errors that human fancy has produced? Is it not better to suspend your conviction than to get mixed up in these seditious and quarrelsome divisions?" (II.12.373). One might assume that Montaigne is paraphrasing Sextus here, but he is not; the emphasis on liberty is his own. Certainty is a form of subjection, whereas remaining "in suspense" lends power and independence to one's judgmental capacities. We retain our liberty, at least in part, by being moderate, temperate, uncertain. As we saw earlier, Montaigne is adamant that we have a right to doubt, a right *not* to know. And in exercising this right we experience cognitive freedom—a means of escape from ideological constraint.

Consider the case of America. Montaigne died a century after Columbus sailed from Spain to the West Indies, but by the 1520s it was already evident that the New World was not merely an archipelago but a colossal landmass, "nearly equal in size to the one we know" (II.12.430). European geographers quickly adjusted to this altered image of the earth, and before long they were assuring Montaigne's contemporaries that "all is now discovered and all is seen" (II.12.430). The indigenous peoples of Australia would have found this an amusing notion; Montaigne clearly did. A thousand years ago, he notes, "it would have been Pyrrhonizing to cast in doubt the science of cosmography, and the opinions that were accepted about it by one and all" (II.12.430). But the same was true in 1580. "Pyrrhonizing," in short, is questioning authority; it is free-thinking. Even in the chapter where he first presents the skepticism of antiquity, Montaigne absorbs this skepticism into his own unique outlook. And what this finally means is that being skeptical and writing essays are intimately related activities. They are not identical, but the latter almost always demands the former as an essential prerequisite.

Late in the chapter "Of Presumption," Montaigne mentions that "irresolution" is one of his predominant traits—indeed that he regards it as a "scar" and "a most harmful failing in negotiating worldly affairs" (II.17.496). But given that the *Essays* urge full disclosure, Montaigne feels obliged to mention his irresolution, and he does so with no attempt to conceal its disfiguring nature. "I do not know which side to take in doubtful matters," he says; "I can easily maintain an opinion, but not choose one" (II.17.496). What he *can* choose, however, is to make a virtue of necessity, and this is what he does: "I keep within me doubt and freedom of choice until the occasion is urgent" (II.17.496). Montaigne's irresolution thus takes on the positive character associated with skepticism and liberty—and it does so precisely at a moment in which he is essaying himself. To essay, then, is to question and doubt; it is to use one's freedom to detach oneself not only from dogmatic convictions but from customary behaviors, habits of thought, and natural inclinations. In the end it is not sustainable, at least as a permanent mode of being conjoined with belief in transcendental realities known solely through revelation and grace. But for Montaigne it is an essential and profoundly desirable component of everyday existence.

Chapter 9
Death and the good life

Just as doubt, for Montaigne, is inseparable from effective, responsible thinking, a steady consideration of death forms part of any life worth living. Montaigne is surprisingly optimistic in his earlier essays about the liberatory effects of inspecting and accepting mortality; later, less confident that we can detach ourselves from the constraints of earthly existence, he remains adamant that death is inextricably bound up with life—indeed that we rub shoulders with death every day. The recurrent misery of kidney stones no doubt contributed to this adjustment of perspective; witness the passage in the *Essays'* final chapter, "Of Experience," where Montaigne writes amusingly of his intellect reminding his imagination that "if you do not embrace death, at least you shake hands with it once a month" (III.13.837). But even in revised sections of Book One, Montaigne argues that if our youthful vitality has left us forever, we cannot consider ourselves fully alive. He also finds the movement from an elderly, diminished life to no life at all less cruel and extreme than the movement from "a flourishing life to a grievous and painful one" (I.20.63). If we die of old age, we have almost certainly been dying for quite some time.

Assuaging our fear of death by contemplating its mystery and inevitability is a recommendation that Montaigne never withdraws. He knows that we are incapable of rehearsing death in the same way we can rehearse military combat or material deprivation, but he says that life itself provides us with means of glimpsing its eventual extinction. One of these means, predictably, is sleep (II.6.268). Another is serious physical injury, and in the chapter "Of Practice" Montaigne relates the story of a near-death experience he underwent sometime in the late 1560s. Riding close to his chateau one afternoon, he was involved in a violent collision with a much larger man on a much larger horse; after being thrown "ten or twelve paces," he lay motionless on the ground, battered and unconscious, with "no more feeling than a log" (II.6.269). Fearing that he might be dead, his servants carried him to the house, and he gradually came to his senses after vomiting a bucketful of blood. In the ensuing days he suffered enormous pain, but he never forgot the sensation of dreamy languor he had felt between the states of stunned oblivion and returning sentience. "It would, in truth, have been a very happy death," he writes, "for the weakness of my understanding kept me from having any judgment of it, and that of my body from having any feeling of it. I was letting myself slip away so gently, so gradually and easily, that I hardly ever did anything with less of a feeling of effort" (II.6.272).

Life, death, and performance

Eager to "familiarize" himself with death (II.6.268), Montaigne had been granted an opportunity to spy at close quarters on his own potential demise, and he did just that. At the same time, however, he knew that each death is unique and that we have little control over the circumstances that present themselves at the end of our lives. Still, he argues, our deaths should be exemplary if possible, or at the very least consistent with our long-term selves (III.12.805). Yet in saying this he raises questions about role play and theatricality that vex his meditations not only on the good death but on the good life as well.

Because human social existence is so heavily scripted, people grow accustomed to playing multiple parts as they move from youth to adulthood and into their later years. Montaigne thus cautions us that we cannot judge a man's happiness "until he has been seen to play the last act of his comedy":

> In everything else there may be sham: the fine reasonings of philosophy may be a mere pose in us; or else our trials, by not testing us to the quick, give us a chance to keep our faces always composed. But in the last scene, between death and ourselves, there is no more pretending; we must talk plain French, we must show what there is that is good and clean at the bottom of the pot. (I.19.55)

Relying as he often does on the ancient metaphor that life is a play, Montaigne complicates his thought by suggesting that in death there can be no performance. Yet the vision of authenticity implied by this comment is routinely contradicted elsewhere in the *Essays*: Montaigne himself has known despicable men who parted from the world in deaths "composed to perfection" (I.19.55).

More fundamentally, however, he appears to be convinced—certainly by the time he writes "Of Repentance"—that other people "do not see you, they guess at you by uncertain conjectures; they see not so much your nature as your art" (III.2.613). If he is right about this, and if his claim pertains to dying as well to living, we may never be able to discern the boundaries between role play and artless existence. Divine omniscience is another matter altogether, and perhaps Montaigne imagines death as a moment of supreme clarity in which self-deception vanishes as people see a God who truly sees them. But given that human judgment is centrally at issue here, the distinction between a person's self-awareness at death and the awareness of others who observe that death continues to trouble Montaigne. It seems improbable, moreover, that hypocrisy and deeply ingrained habits of truth-evasion simply disappear during the final scene of life: people commonly believe that the bottom of their pot is far cleaner than it actually is. At all events, Montaigne makes clear that allegations of authenticity with respect to living and dying are highly susceptible to skeptical investigation.

He displays similar skepticism in advising that we resist fixity and open ourselves instead to adaptive flexibility. "We must not nail ourselves down so firmly to our humors and dispositions," he says. "Our principal talent is the ability to apply ourselves to various practices. It is existing, but not living, to keep ourselves bound and obliged by necessity to a single course" (III.3.621). At first glance, such a claim might seem to conflict with Montaigne's arguments about the "ruling pattern," or *forme maistresse*, that we discover in ourselves as we mature in self-knowledge (III.2.615). But to insist that there are moments when we should feign ignorance or drink to excess despite our commitments to honesty or temperance is hardly to deny that we have core traits and inclinations (III.3.624, I.26.123–24). Knowing our ruling pattern, we become better at parting from it when doing so is the best response to specific circumstances. Role play is thus crucial not only to successful social engagement but to refining our self-recognition, enhancing our self-creation, and acknowledging the parochial aspects of all human interaction.

Pascal famously suggests in his *Pensées* that people can develop sincere Christian faith by behaving as though they have such faith. "Follow the way by which [many Christians] began: they acted as if they believed, took holy water, had masses said, etc. This will make you believe naturally and mechanically." Conscious performance, by this logic, can lead to authentic and nonperformative faith. Readers have often considered this a scandalous recommendation, but Montaigne might well have agreed with Pascal. Not that he ever downplays the reality and importance of distinctions between seeming and being; as he writes in a late addition to "Of the Resemblance of Children to Fathers," "philosophy trains us for ourselves, not for others; for being, not for seeming" (II.37.577; cf. III.10.773–74). But seeming is also a form of being, just as acting is a form of existing. Montaigne alludes to the Roman rhetorician Quintilian in this regard: "having undertaken to arouse some passion in others, [he] espoused it himself to the point of being overcome not only by tears but by the pallor of countenance and bearing of a man really overwhelmed with grief" (III.4.637).

Though easily abused, performance and role play can nonetheless serve as useful strategies within an assemblage of identity tactics about which Montaigne is deeply curious and through which he advances his account of selves in the world—above all his own. "The best of my bodily qualities," he tells us, "is that I am flexible and not very stubborn. I have inclinations that are more personal and customary, and more agreeable to me than others; but with very little effort I turn away from them, and easily slip into the opposite habit" (III.13.830).

Self-deception: ideological and otherwise

Never one to lavish praise on habitual or customary behavior, Montaigne still recognizes that such behavior has its merits: we can make a habit, for instance, of changing our habits. But he knows as well that the habitual and the customary are profound allies of ideological indoctrination, and he routinely depicts them as obstacles in the path of productive thought. "Wherever I want to turn, I have to force some barrier of custom, so carefully has it blocked all our approaches" (I.36.166). As a consequence, demystification becomes one of his standard practices in the *Essays*, and dismantling supposed truths one of his key forms of success: "it is easy to see that it is custom that makes impossible for us what is not impossible in itself" (I.36.167).

As he tells us in "Of Friendship," Montaigne had been exposed during his youth to La Boétie's *Discourse on Voluntary Servitude*, and it may have been partly through reading this treatise that he developed a heightened sensitivity to the idea of cultural habituation as "Circe's drink, which varies our nature as it sees fit" (III.13.827). Claiming that tyrants are enabled to govern because the general populace consents to its own subjection, La Boétie argues that while tyranny is neither necessary nor inevitable, people accept it through a collective failure to recognize their liberty and an unwillingness to suppose that social structures might be altered; a withdrawal of consent, after all, might lead to significant political reformation. Not surprisingly, La Boétie praises the assassination of Julius Caesar by Brutus and other defenders of the Roman Republic, and readers familiar with Shakespeare will be reminded of Cassius's succinct diagnosis: "The fault, dear Brutus, is not in our stars, / But in ourselves, that we are underlings."

Montaigne, however, is ultimately more interested in individual self-deception than in collective indoctrination. He knows the Machiavellian hypothesis that religion was invented to coerce people into awed and fearful obedience (e.g., II.12.414, II.16.477, III.10.769), and he alludes as well to the Platonic view that since it is easy "to imprint all sorts of phantasms on the human mind," rulers should deceive people with "profitable lies" rather than with useless or harmful fictions: "[Plato] says quite shamelessly in his *Republic* that it is often necessary to trick men for their own good" (II.12.379–80). But the narcotic delusions sponsored by hope, fear, vanity, and desire repeatedly arrest his attention. He opens his chapter "Of Presumption" with a brief but perceptive analysis of inflated self-worth (II.17.478), and in "On Some Verses of Virgil" he argues that willful refusal to face our vicious habits gets in the way of self-understanding and self-development: "Those who hide [vice] from others ordinarily hide it from themselves. And they do not consider it covered up enough if they themselves see it; they withdraw and disguise it from their own conscience" (III.5.642). Montaigne, by contrast, is profoundly and permanently aware that he can be deceived (II.8.287), that his opinions are disturbingly changeable (II.12.423, II.17.496), and that he is "full of inanity and nonsense" (III.9.766)—an imperfect man with "a commonplace soul" (I.39.182). But his inestimable compensating advantage is that he welcomes every opportunity to acknowledge and explore his failings.

Some readers today might argue that Montaigne is just as susceptible to religious and political indoctrination as he believes his contemporaries often are. In the "Apology for Raymond Sebond," for example, he offers a critique of the widespread human failure to ascertain whether alleged truths are in fact true; people "dispute only about the branches" rather than examining the roots and the trunk, where "fault and weakness" lie (II.12.403). Yet in the same chapter, just a few pages earlier, he confidently claims that "it is far from honoring him who made us, to honor him whom we have made" (II.12.395). However brilliant an assessment of anthropocentric imagining this is—however valuable a debunking of ideological illusion—Montaigne's assertion of simple faith in God ignores the very advice he has urged upon others: to ask whether specific pronouncements correspond accurately to the realities they purport to describe (II.12.403; cf. III.11.785). What we see here, then, may be voluntary servitude of a different sort, and Montaigne may be an inadvertent target of a reproach he thinks he has avoided: "Men put greater faith in those things that they do not understand. By a twist of the human mind, obscure things are more readily believed" (III.11.789).

But Montaigne's existence and outlook are nearly five centuries removed from our own, and despite the extraordinary assistance he lends us through his *Essays*, no one—not even those with the greatest aptitude for historical imagining—can enter his mind or approach important questions from within the same framework of presuppositions that guide his thought. He stands among the foremost inquirers of Renaissance Europe, and his readiness to suspend judgment and remain agnostic on a wide range of topics will never cease to be remarkable, but like everyone else he is influenced by prevailing conceptual paradigms; there are realms into which his skepticism does not extend. We have touched already on one of the most crucial of these—gender—and Judeo-Christian scripture is another. "Divine doctrine," Montaigne observes in "Of Prayers," is best left undiluted by "human reasonings"; "[she] keeps her rank better apart, as queen and mistress" (I.56.234). Credulity is therefore less at issue here than are the presumed structures of reality on which Montaigne grounds his meditations, and in the end it is by no means unthinkable that Montaignian doubt is underwritten by Montaignian faith.

Embodiment

What constitutes Montaignian faith nonetheless amounts to an idiosyncratic collection of emphases, avowals, and omissions. Montaigne speaks of God and the soul hundreds of times in the *Essays*, and he displays intense interest in repentance, prayer, conscience, comparative devotional practice, and religious belief more generally. Topics such as providence, grace, sin, holiness, heresy, prophecy, and the miraculous also figure significantly in his ruminations. But he refers to Jesus only six times, and allusions to salvation, damnation, hell, resurrection, the Holy Spirit, and other constituent elements of Christian thought occur with extreme infrequency. As for the conventional Christian subordination of the body to the soul, the *Essays'* cumulative testimony leaves little doubt that Montaigne regarded such hierarchical prescriptiveness as detrimental to the well-being of most humans.

"I hate to have people order us to keep our minds in the clouds while our bodies are at table" (III.13.850). Drawn from "Of Experience," this remark alludes not only to Christian teaching but to a broader Western tradition of maligning or demonizing the body, and it illustrates a pronounced tendency of Montaigne's later thought. Yet even in the 1580 version of "On the Education of Children," Montaigne insists that boys require a well-rounded upbringing, since it is neither a body nor a soul that is being

formed, but a man: "these parts must not be separated" (I.26.122).
And by the time he writes "On Some Verses of Virgil," Montaigne
is adamant that the body and the mind are best understood as
existing in symbiosis; they must come to one another's aid as often
as is necessary. Exuberant youthful bodies need rational
management, and morose elderly minds can be soothed and
relaxed through physical pleasure. "May we not say that there is
nothing in us during this earthly imprisonment that is purely
either corporal or spiritual, that we do wrong to tear apart a living
man, and that it seems somewhat reasonable that we should
behave as favorably toward the use of pleasure as we do toward
pain?" (III.5.681).

We know from previous chapters that Montaigne emphasizes the
inescapably "physical" aspects of human nature (III.8.710); John
Florio captures this emphasis memorably in his Elizabethan
translation of the *Essays*: "It is man with whom we have always
to do, whose condition is marvelouslie corporall." Few readers,
then, will be surprised that Montaigne condemns ascetic and
self-denying behavior. Insofar as it is our lot to be embodied
creatures, despising our embodiment is perverse as well as absurd.
"Alas, poor man! You have enough necessary ills without
increasing them by your invention, and you are miserable enough
by nature without being so by art" (III.5.670). For Montaigne,
imagining that the human condition is inherently shameful and
that it calls for regimes of self-abasement is tantamount to
insulting God by rejecting his gift of existence (III.13.855). People
who behave this way "denature" themselves (III.5.670); they deny
their evident commonality with nonhuman animals. "It is a
malady peculiar to man, and not seen in any other creature, to
hate and disdain himself" (II.3.254).

But in addition to being unnatural, ungodly, and ungrateful,
ascetic renunciation is also bad for one's health. And few things
are more important to the *Essays*' author. Defining health as
"maintaining my accustomed state without disturbance"

(III.13.827), Montaigne tells us in "Of Practice" that he has enjoyed "perfect and entire" well-being for many years (II.6.268). Only in his later forties did he first experience the torment of the stone, and even then his activities were minimally curtailed: a day or two of acute suffering enabled him to return to his normal vigorous life (III.13.838). Indeed, the transactional quality of Montaigne's ailment does not escape his attention, and while he remains deeply skeptical about the likelihood of a medical cure, he implies that he would endure "the most painful cauteries and incisions" if they might ensure his recovery (II.37.580). "Health," he says, "is a precious thing, and the only one, in truth, which deserves that we employ in its pursuit not only time, sweat, trouble, and worldly goods, but even life, inasmuch as without it life comes to be painful and oppressive" (II.37.580). Precisely what Montaigne means by trading life for health is open to debate, and we are perhaps reminded of his last-gasp strategy of defending Raymond Sebond against rational critique by impugning the validity of all human reasoning. But that health "should be our chief consideration" (I.39.181) remains a claim to which Montaigne almost always extends unqualified endorsement.

Accepting the lives we have

Given Montaigne's celebration of human embodiment, his critique of ascetic behavior, his contempt for medical practice, and his judgment that people have more in common with "the other animals" than they typically acknowledge (II.12.358), we may be tempted to sketch the outlines of a Montaignian worldview that can be extrapolated from scattered passages in the *Essays*. But as most scholars would agree, clarifying Montaigne in such a way would be misleading because the essayist so frequently shifts, adjusts, and contradicts his opinions. In the end it is better to speak of a constellation of major Montaignian attitudes than to suggest that Montaigne presents a systematic and internally consistent account of human life on earth.

"Desires are either natural and necessary, like eating and drinking; or natural and not necessary, like intercourse with females; or neither natural nor necessary. Of this last type are nearly all those of men; they are all superfluous and artificial. For it is marvelous how little Nature needs to be content, how little she has left us to desire" (II.12.346). So notes Montaigne in the earliest text of the "Apology," and despite his transparent assumption that the *Essays* will be read by heteronormative men, we see that even in the 1570s he thinks that genuine human desires, male and female alike, are relatively minimal and that Nature has provided for almost all of them. We should thus conform our desires to our native condition rather than allow their indiscriminate proliferation, which can only lead to unhappiness.

Montaigne never veers from this counsel. His sense of the non-exceptionality of human beings—of their existence along a continuum with nonhuman animals—goes a great way toward diminishing anthropocentric hubris and displacing *Homo sapiens* from the center of the cosmos. A Copernican revolution of sorts, this view comes close to conflating Nature with God, although Montaigne would surely insist on a difference between secondary and primary causation. But if it is true that "Nature has made us a present of a broad capacity for entertaining ourselves apart, and often calls us to do so, to teach us that we owe ourselves in part to society, but in the best part to ourselves" (II.18.504), natural apprehension is presumably aligned with divine desire in nudging us toward self-sufficiency. And if, in addition, Nature can aid us in learning how to die (I.20.63, III.12.804), distinguishing what we need from what we want (III.10.771), and recognizing how "amply furnished" we are for all necessary activities (II.12.333), thanking God for our existence amounts to thanking Nature too. "I accept with all my heart and with gratitude what Nature has done for me," writes Montaigne; "I love life and cultivate it just as God has been pleased to grant it to us" (III.13.854–55). This attitude of calm, measured acceptance pervades much of Book Three and above all its marvelous concluding chapter.

Montaigne on the good life

"Popular opinion is wrong: it is much easier to go along the sides, where the outer edge serves as a limit and a guide, than by the middle way, wide and open, and to go by art than by nature; but it is also much less noble and less commendable. Greatness of soul is not so much pressing upward and forward as knowing how to set oneself in order and circumscribe oneself. It regards as great whatever is adequate, and shows its elevation by liking moderate things better than eminent ones. There is nothing so beautiful and legitimate as to play the man well and properly, no knowledge so hard to acquire as the knowledge of how to live this life well, and naturally; and the most barbarous of our maladies is to despise our being.... It is an absolute perfection and virtually divine to know how to enjoy our being rightfully. We seek other conditions because we do not understand the use of our own, and go outside ourselves because we do not know what it is like inside. Yet there is no use mounting on stilts, for on stilts we must still walk on our own legs. And on the loftiest throne in the world we are still sitting only on our own rump. The most beautiful lives, to my mind, are those that conform to the common human pattern, with order, but without miracle and without eccentricity" (III.13.852, III.13.857).

But there is a crucial caveat. Because Montaigne rejects those views of the good life that ask us to behave in ways that few of us can truly behave, acceptance must always lie fully within our power. Capitulation is not enough. One of the governing ideas of the *Essays* is that while freedom is an evident attribute of human life, the freedom we enjoy is curbed by multiple constraints, so it makes perfect sense that Montaigne would pose the following question: "Is it wrong of [man] not to do what it is impossible for him to do?" (III.9.758). As this question can be rationally answered only in the negative, we are inevitably drawn back to Montaigne's unflinching claim in "Of Repentance" that "My actions are in order and conformity with what I am and with my condition. I can do no better" (III.2.617). At the same time, however, the *Essays* make it clear that we still have sufficient freedom to observe and examine ourselves, to be honest about our thoughts and behavior, to enjoy ourselves without embarrassment even as we engage in modest self-cultivation, and to love the lives we have.

Among the primary traits Montaigne identifies in the Tupinamba natives of Brazil is a "knowledge of how to enjoy their condition happily and be content with it" (I.31.156). Not surprisingly, he later recommends this knowledge to all of us: "It is an absolute perfection and virtually divine to know how to enjoy our being rightfully" (III.13.857). And one of the best ways of approaching such enjoyment is being alert to the moment at hand:

> When I walk alone in a beautiful orchard, if my thoughts have been dwelling on extraneous incidents for some part of the time, for some other part I bring them back to the walk, to the orchard, to the sweetness of this solitude, and to me. Nature has observed this principle like a mother, that the actions she has enjoined upon us for our need should also give us pleasure; and she invites us to them not only through reason, but also through appetite. (III.13.850)

From a Montaignian perspective, attentiveness of this sort is another form of behavioral adjustment that humans are readily capable of enacting. Despite our undeniable frailties—our ignorance, our inconstancy, and our tendencies toward intolerance, delusion, cruelty, and ludicrous presumption—we also possess the inner resources necessary for achieving peace of mind. "We are each richer than we think," says Montaigne (III.12.794), but we too often fail to discover that this is so.

10. The statue of Montaigne in Paris, located in the Place Paul-Painlevé between the Sorbonne and the Musée de Cluny. Based on a stone sculpture by Paul Landowski, this bronze replica retains the familiar neck ruff but dispenses with the hat, providing a particularly genial image of Montaigne.

Final words

No writer can please all readers, and Montaigne is no exception. A man who thinks it appropriate to reveal his sexual and excretory preferences will always seem insufficiently high-minded to some, and others will find little charm in such claims as "I love rain and mud like a duck" (III.9.744). Montaigne's frequent display of his extensive reading will likewise alienate a portion of his audience, as will his acute, unconventional intelligence. Brilliantly perceptive thought expressed in vivid prose with unapologetic independence is an exquisite commodity—but it is not for every market.

As an "ignorant inquirer" (III.2.612) who sets out to observe himself and test his judgment against the urgings of custom, reason, authority, experience, and learned opinion, Montaigne holds a unique place in literary and intellectual history. If not the founder of the essay, he is its first great exponent and its most extraordinary practitioner. In his genial, haphazard fashion, he exposes our pretensions without stirring our self-hatred; no one can bruise and heal our self-esteem in quite the same way. He does not presume to teach, but he nonetheless encourages us to live our lives honestly, openly, and mindfully, alert to social standards without according them undue reverence. And when he says that it is better to walk in the middle of life's road than to hover near its edges (III.13.852), he means that we can draw on our own natural endowments as we move toward deeper self-knowledge and greater self-reliance. If attending to his life was Montaigne's trade and art, his book endures as an incomparable legacy for our own essays at living.

References

Preface

"More books about books": *The Complete Works of Montaigne*, trans.
Donald M. Frame (Stanford, CA: Stanford University Press, 1958),
Book III, ch. 13, 818. Unless otherwise noted, quotations from
Montaigne's *Essays*, *Travel Journal*, and correspondence are
drawn from Frame's excellent translation; I use in-text citation
hereafter, referring sequentially to book, chapter, and page number
(e.g., "III.13.818" for the quotation just cited). On a few occasions I
have made minor alterations to Frame, usually based on the
revised scholarly edition of the "Bordeaux Copy" of Montaigne's
Essays that appeared after Frame's translation had been published:
Pierre Villey and V.-L. Saulnier, eds., *Les Essais de Michel de
Montaigne*, 3 vols. (Paris: Presses universitaires de France, 1965;
repr. 1978, 1992]). I refer to this edition as "Villey-Saulnier."

Chapter 1

"Truth is truth": *Measure for Measure*, 5.1.50–51. All Shakespearean
quotations are drawn from *The Norton Shakespeare*, ed. Stephen
Greenblatt et al., 3rd ed. (New York: Norton, 2016). "Opuscules":
Villey-Saulnier, 413; Frame's rendition, "Moral Essays" (II.10.300),
misses Montaigne's point about the brevity of Plutarch's pieces.
Francis Bacon, *Francis Bacon: A Critical Edition*, ed. Brian Vickers
(Oxford: Oxford University Press, 1996), 677–78. Ralph Waldo
Emerson, "Montaigne; or the Skeptic" (1845), in *Selections from
Ralph Waldo Emerson*, ed. Stephen Whicher (Boston: Houghton

Mifflin, 1957), 290–93. Marie Le Jars de Gournay, *Preface to the Essays of Michel de Montaigne by His Adoptive Daughter*, trans. and ed. Richard Hillman and Colette Quesnel (Tempe, AZ: Medieval & Renaissance Texts & Studies, 1998), 31. Sir William Cornwallis, *Essayes*, ed. Don Cameron Allen (Baltimore: Johns Hopkins University Press, 1946), 42. William Walwyn, *The Writings of William Walwyn*, ed. Jack R. McMichael and Barbara Taft (Athens University of Georgia Press, 1989), 399–400. Blaise Pascal, *Pensées*, ed. and trans. Roger Ariew (Indianapolis: Hackett, 2005), 190. Voltaire, *Lettres Philosophiques*, in *Mélanges*, ed. Jacques Van den Heuvel (Paris: Gallimard, 1961), 127 (Voltaire responds in Letter 25 to various passages in the *Pensées* of Pascal). William Hazlitt, *The Complete Works of William Hazlitt in Twenty-One Volumes*, ed. P. P. Howe (London: J. M. Dent and Sons, 1930–34), 6:92. Friedrich Nietzsche, "Schopenhauer as Educator," in *Unmodern Observations*, ed. and trans. William Arrowsmith (New Haven, CT: Yale University Press, 1990), 171. Virginia Woolf, "Montaigne," in *The Common Reader*, ed. Andrew McNeillie (New York: Harcourt, 1984), 58, 64. T. S. Eliot, "The *Pensées* of Pascal," in *Selected Essays* (New York: Harcourt, Brace, & World, 1950), 362–63. André Gide, "Montaigne" (1939), trans. Dorothy Bussy, repr. *Yale Review* 89, no. 1 (2001): 53–71, here, 57. Stefan Zweig, *Montaigne*, trans. Will Stone (London: Pushkin Press, 2015), 52.

Chapter 2

On the correspondence of Madame de Montaigne with her spiritual director, see Madeleine Lazard, *Michel de Montaigne* (Paris: Fayard, 1992), 150–51. "In the year of our Lord": Philippe Desan, *Montaigne: A Life*, trans. Steven Rendall and Lisa Neal (Princeton, NJ: Princeton University Press, 2017), 197. On Montaigne's diplomatic ambitions, see Desan, 222–53; on his public life more broadly, chapters 2, 4–5, and 7–9 of Desan's detailed biography are indispensable. Cf. George Hoffmann, *Montaigne's Career* (Oxford: Clarendon Press, 1998), especially chapter 6. Donald Frame's study is also well worth reading: *Montaigne: A Biography* (New York: Harcourt, Brace & World, 1965). The passage from "Of Prayers" is drawn from M. A. Screech, trans., *Michel de Montaigne: The Complete Essays* (Harmondsworth: Penguin, 1991), 355–57; cf. Frame, trans., *Complete Works*, I.56.229–31. The possibly apocryphal story of Montaigne's death derives from a letter by his friend Estienne Pasquier (*Les lettres d'Estienne Pasquier*, 3 vols. [Paris: L. Sonnius, 1619], 2:377). The Montaigne Project website at the University of Chicago includes an extremely useful multicolored digital version of the Villey-Saulnier edition: A-text passages of the *Essais* appear in black, B-text passages in blue, and C-text passages in orange. There are also links to high-quality photographic images of all pages in the Bordeaux Copy.

Chapter 3

"The school of Montaigne" alludes to the title of Warren Boutcher's masterful study of the genesis and reception of the *Essays* within a European social network concerned with the training of liberal minds: *The School of Montaigne in Early Modern Europe*, 2 vols. (Oxford: Oxford University Press, 2017). Johnson: see James Boswell, *The Life of Samuel Johnson* (London: Oxford University Press, 1960), 303–4. Translations of *une forme maistresse* (Villey-Saulnier, 811): John Florio, trans., *The Essayes of Montaigne* (London: 1603), 488; J. M. Cohen, trans., *Montaigne's Essays* (Harmondsworth: Penguin, 1958), 243; M. A. Screech, trans., *The Complete Essays* (Harmondsworth: Penguin, 1991), 914. For a discussion of the *forme maistresse* and related topics: R. A. Sayce, *The Essays of Montaigne: A Critical Exploration* (London: Weidenfeld and Nicolson, 1972), 113–59. On Montaigne's uses of his reading, see Peter Mack, *Reading and Rhetoric in Montaigne and Shakespeare* (London: Bloomsbury, 2010). Quotations from Erasmus: Erasmus, *On Education for Children*, in *The Erasmus Reader*, ed. Erika Rummel (Toronto: University of Toronto Press, 1990), 82, 84, 90, 94.

Chapter 4

For Florio on Montaigne's misogyny, see John Florio, trans., *The Essayes of Montaigne* (London: 1603), sig. R2^v. See also Ullrich Langer, *Perfect Friendship: Studies in Literature and Moral Philosophy from Boccaccio to Corneille* (Geneva: Librairie Droz, 1994), for a valuable overview of Renaissance ideas of friendship along with perceptive commentary on Montaigne and La Boétie.

Chapter 5

For a Marxist critique of Montaigne's withdrawal, see Max
Horkheimer, "Montaigne and the Function of Skepticism" (1938),
in *Between Philosophy and Social Science*, trans. G. Frederick
Hunter et al. (Cambridge, MA: MIT Press, 1993), 265–311.
Shakespeare's *As You Like It*: 2.7.139–40. Hoffmann, *Montaigne's
Career*, 62. Francis Bacon, *The New Organon*, ed. Fulton Anderson
(Indianapolis: Bobbs-Merrill, 1960), 47–66.

Chapter 6

Frame often capitalizes "Nature" in his translation of the *Essays*,
particularly when Montaigne uses the word as a personified
abstraction; in French editions of the *Essais* the word is capitalized
far less frequently. The date of Montaigne's conversation with
Tupinamba natives has recently been contested by Philippe Desan
in his biography of the essayist; Desan argues that Montaigne
spoke with these natives not in 1562 but in 1565—and in Bordeaux
rather than in Rouen (*Montaigne: A Life*, 159–75). The extract
from the *Requerimiento* is drawn from Patricia Seed, *Ceremonies of
Possession in Europe's Conquest of the New World, 1492–1640*
(Cambridge: Cambridge University Press, 1995), 69.

Chapter 7

"Give unto Caesar": Matt. 22:21. Cf. Mark 12:13–17, Luke 20:20–26,
Rom. 13:1–7, Titus 1:3. "Providence": according to the two-volume
Concordance des Essais de Montaigne prepared by Roy E. Leake
(Geneva: Librairie Droz, 1981), Montaigne uses the word
providence just six times. "Incorrigibly plural": from "Snow," a
poem by Louis MacNeice.

Chapter 8

Although Montaigne never makes a case for external-world
skepticism, he comes close to establishing the opening premises of
this case. See his comment in "Of Democritus and Heraclitus":
"Things in themselves may have their own weights and measures
and qualities; but once inside, within us, [the soul] allots them

their qualities as she sees fit" (I.50.220). Montaigne is not suggesting that the external world does not exist, but his supposition that we lack reliable access to that world through sense perception is a standard step toward such skepticism; cf. the "Apology" (II.12.451–55). Shakespeare's *Hamlet*: 1.5.168–69. Among the readers who have questioned the sincerity of Montaigne's professions of faith, see, e.g., Hugo Friedrich, *Montaigne*, trans. Dawn Eng (Berkeley: University of California Press, 1991), 26, 94–95, 104–5; André Gide, "Montaigne" (1939), repr. *Yale Review* 89, no. 1 (2001): 63–66; R. A. Sayce, *The Essays of Montaigne*, 228; and David Wootton, *The Invention of Science: A New History of the Scientific Revolution* (New York: Harper Collins, 2015), 559. Marie de Gournay, in her preface to the 1595 *Essais*, emphasizes Montaigne's devout Catholicism (*Preface to the Essays of Michel de Montaigne by His Adoptive Daughter*, 54–57). Sextus Empiricus, *Outlines of Scepticism*, ed. and trans. Julia Annas and Jonathan Barnes, 2nd ed. (Cambridge: Cambridge University Press, 2000), 9, 143. Cicero, *The Nature of the Gods*, trans. P. G. Walsh (Oxford: Oxford University Press, 1998), 109, 113. Charles-Augustin Sainte-Beuve, *Port-Royal*, 7 vols. (Paris: Hachette, 1922–25), 2:395–453. On "free-thinking," see Richard Scholar's excellent study, *Montaigne and the Art of Free-Thinking* (Oxford: Peter Lang, 2010). Sextus Empiricus, *Outlines*, 3–4.

Chapter 9

Pascal: *Pensées*, 214. "Mechanically" strikes many readers as an incongruous term in this context, but it is a legitimate way of rendering the French *vous abêtira* ("you will become stupid" [i.e., dull, unthinking, bestial]). Pascal argues, in short, that acting as though you believe will make you more like a nonhuman animal: your belief will become natural and instinctual. For La Boétie's treatise, see the recent English translation by James B. Atkinson and David Sices, eds., *Michel de Montaigne, Selected Essays, and Étienne de La Boétie, Discourse on Voluntary Servitude* (Indianapolis: Hackett, 2012), 284–312. Cassius's speech to Brutus: *Julius Caesar*, 1.2.140–41. I take the term "Machiavellian hypothesis" from Stephen Greenblatt, *Shakespearean Negotiations* (Berkeley: University of California Press, 1988), 24. "*Men put...readily believed*": Frame italicizes these sentences because they are classical quotations; the first has not been convincingly traced, while the second derives from Tacitus's *Histories*, I.22. Florio's phrase "marvelouslie corporall" appears on p. 557 of his 1603 London edition of the *Essayes*.

Further reading

Recommended readings from Montaigne's *Essays* for each chapter of this book

I refer here to the titles given by Donald Frame to individual essays by Montaigne, but I also list these essays' book and chapter numbers (e.g., I.8 or III.2), since translators other than Frame sometimes offer different renditions of the original French titles.

Chapter 1

"To the Reader," "Of Idleness" (I.8), "Of Democritus and Heraclitus" (I.50), "Of Practice" (II.6), "Of Giving the Lie" (II.18), "Of Repentance" (III.2)

Chapter 2

"Of the Education of Children" (I.26), "Of Friendship" (I.28), "Of Practice" (II.6), "Of Presumption" (II.17), "Of Physiognomy" (III.12); also Montaigne's *Travel Journal*

Chapter 3

"Of Pedantry" (I.25), "Of the Education of Children" (I.26), "Of the Affection of Fathers for Their Children" (II.8), "Of Books" (II.10), "Of Repentance" (III.2), "Of Three Kinds of Association" (III.3), "Of the Art of Discussion" (III.8)

Chapter 4

"Of the Power of the Imagination" (I.21), "Of Friendship" (I.28), "Of Moderation" (I.30), "Of the Affection of Fathers for Their Children" (II.8), "That Our Desire Is Increased by Difficulty" (II.15), "Of Three Good Women" (II.35), "Of Three Kinds of Association" (III.3), "Of Diversion" (III.4), "On Some Verses of Virgil" (III.5)

Chapter 5

"That Intention Is Judge of Our Actions" (I.7), "That to Philosophize Is to Learn to Die" (I.20), "Of Custom, and Not Easily Changing an Accepted Law" (I.23), "Of Solitude" (I.39), "Of the Inconsistency of Our Actions" (II.1), "Of Repentance" (III.2), "Of Three Kinds of Association" (III.3), "Of Husbanding Your Will" (III.10)

Chapter 6

"To the Reader," "Of Cannibals" (I.31), "Of Conscience" (II.5), "Of Cruelty" (II.11), "Cowardice, Mother of Cruelty" (II.27), "Of Virtue" (II.29), "Of Coaches" (III.6)

Chapter 7

"Of Custom, and Not Easily Changing an Accepted Law" (I.23), "It Is Folly to Measure the True and False by Our Own Capacity" (I.27), "Of Ancient Customs" (I.49), "Of the Inconsistency of Our Actions" (II.1), "An Apology for Raymond Sebond" (II.12), "Of a Monstrous Child" (II.30), "Defense of Seneca and Plutarch" (II.32), "Of Vanity" (III.9), "Of Cripples" (III.11), "Of Experience" (III.13)

Chapter 8

"It Is Folly to Measure the True and False by Our Own Capacity" (I.27), "Of the Uncertainty of Our Judgment" (I.47), "Of Democritus and Heraclitus" (I.50), "Of Prayers" (I.56), "An Apology for Raymond Sebond" (II.12), "Of Presumption" (II.17), "Of Cripples" (III.11)

Chapter 9

"That Our Happiness Must Not Be Judged until after Our Death"
(I.19), "That to Philosophize Is to Learn to Die" (I.20), "Of Prayers"
(I.56), "Of Age" (I.57), "A Custom of the Island of Cea" (II.3), "Of
Practice" (II.6), "Of the Resemblance of Children to Fathers"
(II.37), "Of Repentance" (III.2), "Of Three Kinds of Association"
(III.3), "On Some Verses of Virgil" (III.5), "Of Vanity" (III.9), "Of
Physiognomy" (III.12), "Of Experience" (III.13)

Selected English translations of Montaigne's *Essays*

Serious students of Montaigne will usually acquire multiple editions of
the *Essays*. For anglophone readers the best complete translations
are those of Donald M. Frame (1958) and M. A. Screech (1991).
Frame's translation, used in this book, has the advantage of
including Montaigne's *Travel Journal* and surviving letters. It was
republished in 2003 (New York: Everyman's Library) but, alas,
with different pagination.

Atkinson, James B., and David Sices, trans. and eds. *Montaigne:
Selected Essays. With La Boétie's Discourse on Voluntary Servitude.*
Indianapolis: Hackett, 2012. [New English translation of eighteen
Montaignian essays along with La Boétie's treatise.]

Cotton, Charles, trans. *Essays of Michael Seigneur de Montaigne in
Three Books.* 3 vols. London: 1685–86. [Replaced John Florio's
Elizabethan translation of the *Essays* with a more sober and
accurate text; served English readers throughout the eighteenth
and nineteenth centuries as the primary means of access to
Montaigne.]

Florio, John, trans. *The Essayes or Morall, Politike and Millitarie
Discourses of Lo[rd] Michaell de Montaigne.* London: 1603. [The
first complete English translation of the *Essays*, published just
eleven years after Montaigne's death; memorably exuberant if not
consistently reliable, and highly influential in English literary
history. Available online at the University of Pennsylvania's
Schoenberg Center for Electronic Text and Image.]

Frame, Donald M., trans. *The Complete Works of Montaigne.* Stanford,
CA: Stanford University Press, 1958. [Unabridged translation of
the *Essays*; also includes Montaigne's *Travel Journal* and extant
correspondence; generally regarded as the translation that best
captures the literary style of Montaigne.]

Greenblatt, Stephen, and Peter G. Platt, eds. *Shakespeare's Montaigne: The Florio Translation of the Essays: A Selection*. New York: New York Review Books, 2014. [Abridged edition of John Florio's translation, with valuable introductory essays by the editors.]

Screech, M. A., trans. *Michel de Montaigne: The Complete Essays*. Harmondsworth: Penguin, 1991. [Often livelier than Donald Frame's translation and lexically precise despite occasional lapses; does not include Montaigne's *Travel Journal*.]

Selected French editions of Montaigne's *Essais*

Balsamo, Jean, Michel Magnien, Catherine Magnien-Simonin, and Alain Legros, eds. *Les Essais*. Bibliothèque de la Pléiade. Paris: Gallimard, 2007. [Text based on the 1595 Paris edition of the *Essais* (prepared in part by Marie de Gournay); does not include strata markers for passages originating in 1580, 1588, and 1595; offers extensive and learned scholarly annotation by the editors.]

Tournon, André, ed. *Essais de Michel de Montaigne*. 3 vols. Paris: Bibliothèque nationale de France, 1998. [Text based on the Bordeaux Copy of the 1588 *Essais*, which was extensively augmented and corrected by Montaigne; Tournon pays scrupulous attention to Montaigne's revisions in punctuation.]

Villey, Pierre, and V.-L. Saulnier, eds. *Les essais de Michel de Montaigne*. 3 vols. Paris: Presses universitaires de France, 1965. Reprinted 1978, 1992. [Text based on the Bordeaux Copy of the 1588 *Essais*; includes valuable appendices regarding Montaigne's library and his early reception in France and elsewhere. Available online at the University of Chicago's *Montaigne Project*.]

Biographies, introductory studies, and overviews of Montaigne

Bakewell, Sarah. *How to Live: Or, A Life of Montaigne in One Question and Twenty Attempts at an Answer*. New York: Other Press, 2010. [Enormously readable account of Montaigne's life, times, and writings.]

Burke, Peter. *Montaigne*. Past Masters Series. Oxford: Oxford University Press, 1981. [Concise overview of Montaigne's life and *Essays*; chapters are organized around Montaigne's attitudes toward subjects of major cultural interest.]

Cave, Terence. *How to Read Montaigne*. London: Granta, 2007. [Brilliant brief treatment of the *Essays* from a cognitive rather than a philosophical perspective; shows through close readings how Montaigne's chapters reflect the "soundings" or trials of thought that enable their composition.]

Desan, Philippe. *Montaigne: A Life*. Translated by Steven Rendall and Lisa Neal. Princeton, NJ: Princeton University Press, 2017. [Immensely detailed biography, with particular attention to Montaigne's political and diplomatic ambitions; situates the *Essays* within this context.]

Frame, Donald M. *Montaigne: A Biography*. New York: Harcourt, Brace & World, 1965. Reprinted San Francisco: North Point Press, 1984. [Excellent and influential biography; probably the best choice for beginning students of Montaigne.]

Miller, James. *Examined Lives: From Socrates to Nietzsche*. New York: Farrar, Straus, and Giroux, 2011. [The chapter on Montaigne is useful, though mistaken in certain details; best read in conjunction with other studies.]

Scholar, Richard. *Montaigne and the Art of Free-Thinking*. Oxford: Peter Lang, 2010. [Outstanding introduction to the *Essays* with particular attention to relations between freedom of thought and the Montaignian essay as a mode of testing our judgment.]

Taylor, Charles. *Sources of the Self: The Making of the Modern Identity*. Cambridge, MA: Harvard University Press, 1989. [Includes a valuable chapter on Montaigne; characterizes the essayist as "an originator of the search for each person's originality" (p. 182).]

Websites, encyclopedias, teaching resources, and reference works

Desan, Philippe, ed. *Dictionnaire de Michel de Montaigne*. 2nd ed. Paris: Honoré Champion, 2007. [Vast collection of entries on people, places, events, books, and themes pertinent to the study of Montaigne; a crucial scholarly resource.]

Desan, Philippe, ed. *The Montaigne Project*. https://montaignestudies. uchicago.edu. [Invaluable website at the University of Chicago, featuring links to digital versions of the *Essays*, a portrait gallery, multiple bibliographies, and information about the scholarly journal *Montaigne Studies*.]

Desan, Philippe. *Portraits à l'essai: iconographie de Montaigne*. Paris: Honoré Champion, 2007. [Best resource for visual representations of Montaigne, including sketches, paintings, engravings, statues, busts, medals, etc.; more than 300 plates, both black-and-white and color.]

Henry, Patrick, ed. *Approaches to Teaching Montaigne's Essays.* New York: Modern Language Association of America, 1994. [Valuable resource for teachers introducing college students to Montaigne.]

Hoffmann, George. Oxford Bibliographies Online: Montaigne. https://oxfordbibliographies.com. [Incisive online bibliographic entries on all aspects of Montaigne's life and writing.]

Marchand, Jean, ed. *Le livre de raison de Montaigne.* Paris: Société des amis de Montaigne, 1948. [Facsimile edition of Montaigne's copy of the 1551 *Ephemeris historica* by Michael Beuther, containing manuscript notes by Montaigne and other family members on births, deaths, travels, visitors to the chateau, etc.]

Selected scholarly monographs and edited collections (see also the citations listed in the References)

Auerbach, Erich. *Mimesis: The Representation of Reality in Western Literature.* Bern: Francke, 1946. Reprinted with translation by Willard R. Trask. Princeton, NJ: Princeton University Press, 2003. [Chapter 12 focuses on "Of Repentance," dealing valuably with Montaigne's style and habits of self-representation, though Auerbach does not discuss the essay's religious or philosophical dimensions.]

Boase, Alan M. *The Fortunes of Montaigne: A History of the Essays in France, 1580–1669.* London: Methuen, 1935. [Valuable account of the reasons behind conflicting early responses to the *Essays*.]

Boutcher, Warren. *The School of Montaigne in Early Modern Europe.* 2 vols. Oxford: Oxford University Press, 2017. [Original, wide-ranging study of Montaigne's place at the center of a European intellectual network focused on the education and training of the nobility; opens new modes of inquiry within literary/cultural interrelations.]

Brahami, Frédéric. *Le scepticisme de Montaigne.* Paris: Presses universitaires de France, 1997. [Treats Montaignian skepticism not as a modification of Pyrrhonism but as a new and generative form of investigation mediated by Montaigne's encounter with Raymond Sebond's treatise.]

Calhoun, Alison. *Montaigne and the Lives of the Philosophers: Life Writing and Transversality in the Essais.* Newark: University of

Delaware Press, 2014. [Intriguing study of Montaigne's orientation toward the teaching of moral philosophy through scrutiny of the lives that philosophers have actually led; emphasis on Montaigne's use of Plutarch and Diogenes Laertius.]

Desan, Philippe, ed. *The Oxford Handbook of Montaigne*. New York: Oxford University Press, 2016. [The most up-to-date general guide to Montaigne: forty-two essays—many of them quite accessible for nonspecialists—on a wide range of topics both historical and thematic.]

Friedrich, Hugo. *Montaigne*. Bern: Francke, 1949. Reprinted, edited by Philippe Desan, translated by Dawn Eng. Berkeley: University of California Press, 1991. [Classic, comprehensive, penetrating study of Montaigne's *Essays*, still very much relevant today.]

Godman, Peter. *The Saint as Censor: Robert Bellarmine between Inquisition and Index*. Leiden: Brill, 2000. [Updates Smith, 1981, with new archival evidence relevant to Montaigne's censorship by Vatican officials; includes a transcription, in Italian, of the comments made by clerics who examined the 1580 *Essais*.]

Green, Felicity. *Montaigne and the Life of Freedom*. Cambridge: Cambridge University Press, 2012. [Revisionist study situating Montaigne's project within practices of self-control inherited from antiquity; takes issue with readings of the *Essays* as a progenitor of modern conceptions of the self.]

Hamlin, William M. *Montaigne's English Journey: Reading the* Essays *in Shakespeare's Day*. Oxford: Oxford University Press, 2013. [Unlike his *Essays*, Montaigne never traveled to England; this study focuses on English readership of the essayist in the early modern era, roughly 1590–1700.]

Hartle, Ann. *Michel de Montaigne: Accidental Philosopher*. Cambridge: Cambridge University Press, 2003. [Sees in Montaigne not so much a skeptic as an original philosopher who incorporates skepticism as one "moment" within a larger and fundamentally dialectical thought progression.]

Hoffmann, George. *Montaigne's Career*. Oxford: Clarendon Press, 1998. [Engrossing study of the essayist's "career"; Montaigne is shown to be enmeshed in multiple social networks as he drafts, publishes, revises, and augments his book.]

Kenny, Neil, Richard Scholar, and Wes Williams, eds. *Montaigne in Transit: Essays in Honour of Ian Maclean*. Cambridge: Legenda, 2016. [Strong collection of articles focused on the "transit" of the

Essays through time and language, with emphasis on questions of genesis, production, diffusion, and reception.]

Langer, Ullrich, ed. *The Cambridge Companion to Montaigne.* Cambridge: Cambridge University Press, 2005. [Eleven excellent essays on central Montaignian themes.]

Langer, Ullrich. *Perfect Friendship: Studies in Literature and Moral Philosophy from Boccaccio to Corneille.* Geneva: Librairie Droz, 1994. [Outstanding study of Renaissance ideas of friendship, with generous attention to Montaigne and La Boétie.]

Larmore, Charles. "Scepticism." In *The Cambridge History of Seventeenth-Century Philosophy*, edited by Daniel Garber and Michael Ayers, vol. 2, 1145–92. Cambridge: Cambridge University Press, 1998. [Lucid, thorough, responsible account of Renaissance skepticism, with detailed and valuable attention to Montaigne.]

Mack, Peter. *Reading and Rhetoric in Montaigne and Shakespeare.* London: Bloomsbury, 2010. [Excellent comparative account of the ways Montaigne and Shakespeare made use of their reading; deeply grounded in Renaissance rhetorical and educational practices.]

Popkin, Richard H. *The History of Scepticism from Savonarola to Bayle.* Oxford: Oxford University Press, 2003. [Final version of an influential study (first published in 1960) of the rediscovery of ancient skepticism in Renaissance Europe; the treatment of Montaigne is now outdated but still useful in articulating a conception of Montaigne-the-skeptic against which later studies often define themselves.]

Quint, David. *Montaigne and the Quality of Mercy: Ethical and Political Themes in the Essais.* Princeton, NJ: Princeton University Press, 1998. [Reads the *Essays* as vitally concerned with the ethical foundations of social and political life; sees mercy as a key value emerging from Montaigne's contemplation of his world.]

Sayce, R. A. *The Essays of Montaigne: A Critical Exploration.* London: Weidenfeld and Nicolson, 1972. [Judicious, balanced assessment of the *Essays*, with attention to the book's place in the literary history of the Renaissance.]

Schacter, Marc. *Voluntary Servitude and the Erotics of Friendship: From Classical Antiquity to Early Modern France.* Aldershot: Ashgate, 2008. [Shows how the *Essays* present useful ways of investigating the interrelations of friendship, textual production, and selfhood.]

Schmitt, Charles B. *Cicero Scepticus: A Study of the Influence of the Academica in the Renaissance*. The Hague: Nijhoff, 1972. [Indispensable account of academic skepticism in early modern Europe; ideally read in conjunction with Popkin, 2003.]

Screech, M. A. *Montaigne and Melancholy: The Wisdom of the Essays*. London: Duckworth, 1983. [Sensitive study of Montaigne's self-diagnosis as melancholic in temperament; the project of the *Essays*, especially its concern with embodiment and moderation, is thus to a significant degree therapeutic.]

Screech, M. A. *Montaigne's Annotated Copy of Lucretius: A Transcription and Study of the Manuscript, Notes, and Pen-Marks*. Geneva: Librairie Droz, 1998. [Fascinating examination of Montaigne's handwritten notes on Lucretius's poem *De rerum natura (On the Nature of Things)*; Montaigne's copy of Lucretius was presumed lost until it surfaced in 1989.]

Shklar, Judith. *Ordinary Vices*. Cambridge, MA: Harvard University Press, 1984. [Views Montaigne as a source of modern liberal values, including abhorrence of cruelty.]

Smith, Malcolm. *Montaigne and the Roman Censors*. Geneva: Librairie Droz, 1981. [Examines the reactions of papal censors to the 1580 edition of the *Essais*, showing how subsequent versions of Montaigne's book take these reactions into account—or ignore them.]

Toulmin, Stephen. *Cosmopolis: The Hidden Agenda of Modernity*. Chicago: University of Chicago Press, 1990. [Locates the origins of intellectual modernity in sixteenth- rather than seventeenth-century Europe; unpersuasively treats Montaigne as broadly representative of Renaissance humanism, but admires the essayist's candor, skepticism, embrace of diversity, and impatience with dogmatic assertion.]

Tournon, André. *La glose et l'essai*. Lyon: Presses universitaires de Lyon, 1983. Revised edition, Paris: Champion, 2000. [Groundbreaking contextualization of the *Essays* within sixteenth-century French legal practices; finds that Montaigne's pre-trial summaries of evidence, pleas, and conflicting testimonials contributed to the open-ended form his essays ultimately took.]

Villey, Pierre. *Les sources et l'évolution des Essais de Montaigne*. 2nd ed. 2 vols. Paris: Hachette, 1933. [Foundational account of Montaigne's use of his literary, historical, and philosophical sources.]

Index

F

G